MACHINIST GRINDER SECOND YEAR MCQ

OBJECTIVE QUESTION ANSWERS

MANOJ DOLE

Digitization is the need of the time. In the future, training in industrial training institutes will need to be conducted using online internet to make training more convenient and easy. E-books containing a set of MCQ questions will be made available to the trainees as they need to be more accustomed to the multiple choice questions MCQ to prepare for the online exams taking place in their industrial training institutes.

With all these factors in mind, Mr. Manoj Madhukar Dole Instructor, Industrial Training Institute, Satara, has written books according to the new annual system and NSQF-5 syllabus. And they've created theoretical mobile apps and blogs to make training easier, and made all these educational materials available for download on the world famous websites Google Play Store, Amazon and Apple Book Store.

The books were published by Hon'ble Joint Director Shri Rajendra Ghume Saheb Regional Office of Vocational Education and Training, Pune on 9/1/2019, at this time Shri Prakash Saigavkar Saheb Principal Government Industrial Training Institute Aundh Pune, Shri Tukaram Misal Saheb Principal Govt. Q. Sanstha Satara, Shri Sachin Dhumal Saheb District Vocational Education and Training Officer Satara, Shri Yatin Pargaonkar Saheb Principal Govt. Q. Sanstha Kolhapur, Shri Vikas Teke Saheb Inspector Vocational Education and Training Regional Office Pune, Palekar Foods Products Pvt. Ltd. Entrepreneurial Chairman of Satara Mr. Nilkanthrao Palekar Saheb, Chairman of Hira Foods Mr. Ibrahim Baba Tamboli Saheb, Mrs. Shalmali Pawar Headmaster Government Technical School Center Satara and other dignitaries were present on the occasion.

Contents

Prologue *vii*

Foreword *ix*

Preface *xi*

Acknowledgements *xiii*

1. Machinist Grinder Second Year Mcq Drawings 1
2. Machinist Grinder Second Year Mcq 28

Prologue

Machinist Grinder Second Year MCQ is a simple Book for ITI Engineering Course Lift and Escalator Mechanic, Second Year, Sem- 3 & 4, Revised NSQ F-5 Syllabus in 2022, It contains objective questions with underlined & bold correct answers MCQ covering all topics including all about the latest & Important about cylindrical and surface grinder, cylindrical bore grinding, cylindrical grinding and honing, finishing angular form, steps, shoulder, compound or double taper, steep taper, lathe centre, plug, Morse taper, Metric taper, center less grinding process, lapping on flat surface, lapping on cylindrical surface and buffing to limit of h5, CNC machine operation like jog, reference edits, MDI, auto mode program, call & entry, simulation, tool offset and changing and developed skill on operating CNC turning centre as per drawing by preparing Part-program, and lots more.

We add new question answers with each new version. Please email us in case of any errors/omissions. This is arguably the largest and best e-Book for All engineering multiple choice questions and answers.

As a student you can use it for your exam prep. This e-Book is also useful for professors to refresh material.

Foreword

Vocational education and training is imparted through the Department of Vocational Education and Training through the Department of Business Education and Business Practical to supply multi-skilled artisans in line with the rapidly growing demand in the industrial sector in the 21st century. All the occupations within the institutions are important, as the trainees from these occupations develop multi-skills as per the demands of the industry.

with the noble intention of making available MCQ e-books suitable for all businesses, considering that all the examinations in all the industries in the industrial sector are conducted online and include MCQ method questions. Mr. Manoj Madhukar Dole has written a very good e-book on MCQ method as per the new annual syllabus. This e-book will definitely be a guide for all the trainees, trainee candidates, training instructors and others concerned.

The author of the book is Mr. Manoj Madhukar Dole, Instructor Gov. ITI Satara has 17 years of training experience. Written as a new annual pattern, this e-book incorporates modern digital QR Code technology to understand the layout, simple language, and simple syntax, diagrams and videos for each subject. So I am sure that this e-book will definitely be useful for in-depth study and exam practice. The work they have done is certainly commendable.

Mr. Tukaram Misal
Principal Government Industrial Training Institute Satara.

Preface

DGET New Delhi and CSTARI Kolkata have been implementing an annual pattern for all businesses in ITI since the August 2018 session. The examination system will also be changed and it will be online from this year and since all the questions are of Objective Type (MCQ), the trainees are in dire need of in-depth study. It is with this in mind that we are delighted to present the books based on the old NIMI pattern and a complete overview of the new annual pattern, and we hope that these books will be a guide for all business directors and trainees. Is.

For writing these books, Johar Awate Saheb, Principal of ITI Akluj. Former Principal of ITI Satara Saigavkar Saheb, Assistant Director Shri Chandrakant Dhekne Saheb Regional Office of Vocational Education and Training, Pune, District Vocational Education and Training Officer Sachin Dhumal Saheb and Headmaster Government Technical School Kendra Shalmali Pawar Madam and son Adhiraj Dole, mother Kusum Dole, I am very grateful to my father Madhukar Dole and wife Ashwini Dole for their special guidance and cooperation from time to time.

Also, in a very short period of time, the book was reviewed by Shri Rajendra Ghume Saheb, Joint Director, Vocational Education and Training Regional Office, Pune, for his invaluable time in publishing the book. I am sincerely grateful for their feedback.

I am grateful to the Instructor of ITI Satara for there continuous support from the very beginning of writing the book.

From this book, I consider myself blessed to have shared my thoughts on e-learning with you. I will not claim that this book is perfect, because considering the perfection, this book is an attempt and is in its infancy. They will be valuable for improvement if they are tested and suggested.

Manoj Dole
Dated 9/1/2019

Acknowledgements

The industrial training and theoretical examination system of our industrial training institutes and these changes have been accepted by the craft instructors and the trainees. Theoretical examinations conducted in your industrial training institutes are also conducted online. Since these examinations are of multiple choice MCQ method, the trainees will need to get more practice of such questions.

With all these considerations in mind, Mr. Manoj Madhukar, Director, Dole Crafts, Katari Industrial Training Institute, Satara, has done a thorough study and with his diligent work and added his keen intellect, according to the new annual system and NSQF-5 syllabus, e-book of Katari and other machine trades. -Book) and they have created mobile apps and blogs on theoretical topics to make training easier and have made all these educational materials available for download on the world famous websites Google Play Store, Amazon and Apple Book Store. Training has been made easier by creating a print version and using advanced techniques like QR Code.

All these educational materials will definitely be a guide for all the trainees for in-depth study and for the craft instructors and other concerned who are imparting vocational training.

CHAPTER ONE

Machinist Grinder Second Year MCQ Drawings

Online Test Exam
ITI Books
CNC Course
AutoCAD CAM
JOB & Apprentice
Online Theory
Computer Course
Trading Course
Web Designing
MSCIT Course
Shopping Business
Internet Business
Remotasks Course
Online Services
Top Sportsmans
Indian Army
Freedom Fighters
Top Scientists
Social Reformers
Motivational Speaker
Top Richest People
Join WhatsApp Group
Join Facebook Group
Like Facebook Page
PAN / Adhar / Licence Passport

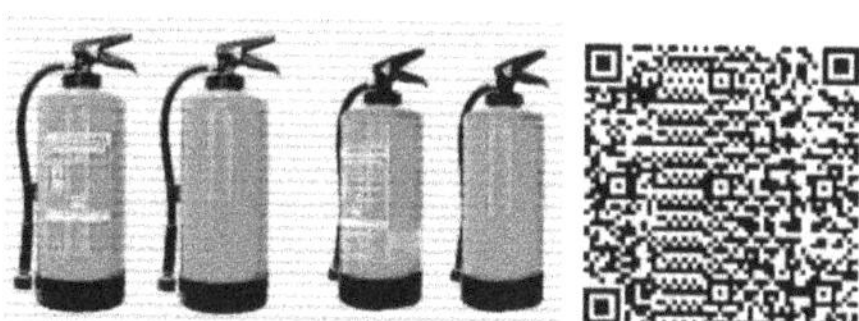

Fire extinguisher

Calliper

Hacksaw frame

Universal surface guage

Hammer

Centre punch

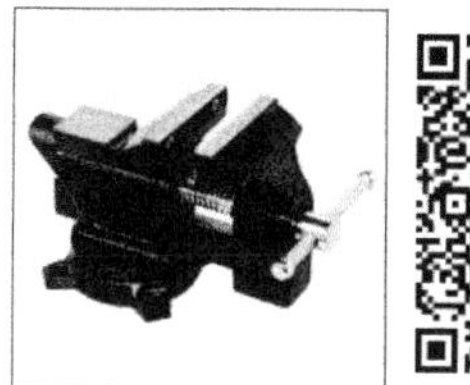

Bench vice

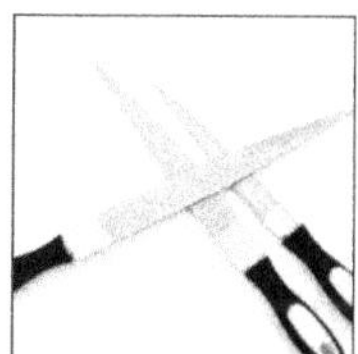

Files

Scraper

Surface Plate

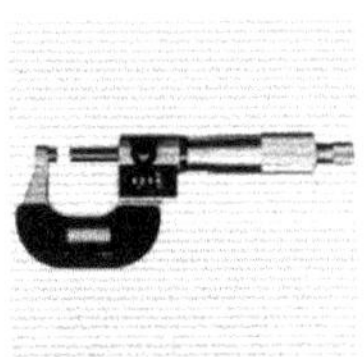

Outside Micrometer

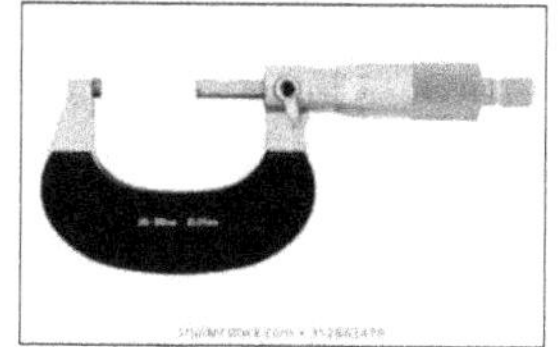 

Micrometer

Depth micrometer

Vernier Calliper

Vernier bevel protractor

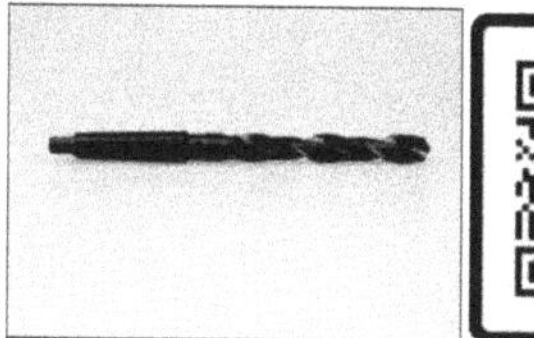

Drilling

Reamer

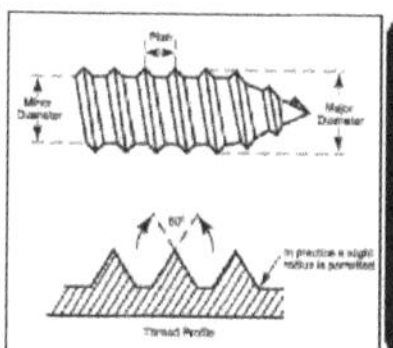

Thread

Tap Die

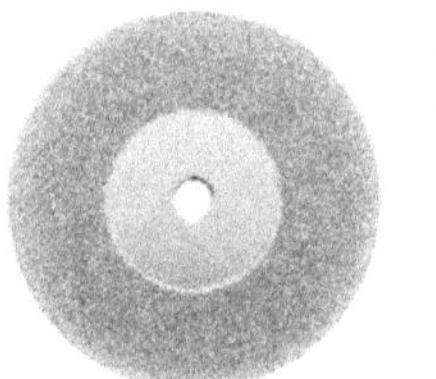

Grinding Wheel

Slip gauge

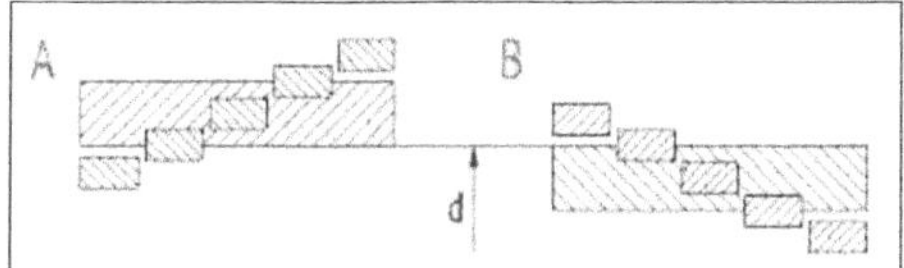

Limit fit tolerance

Lathe Machine

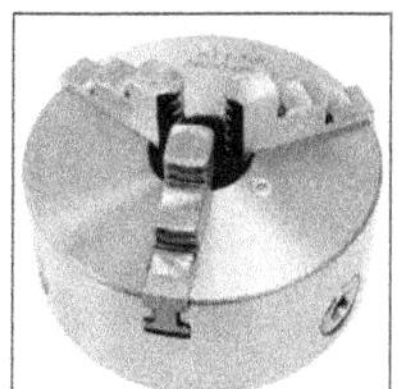

Lathe chuck

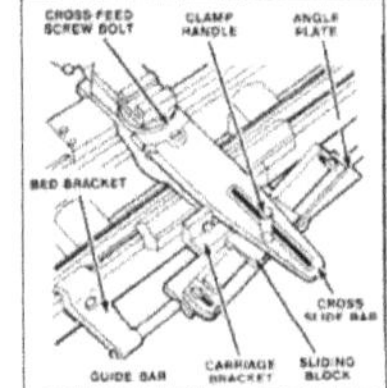

Taper turning attachment

taper ring gauge

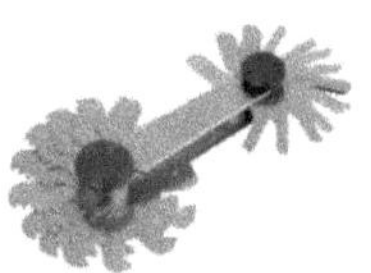

screw pitch gauge

Gear

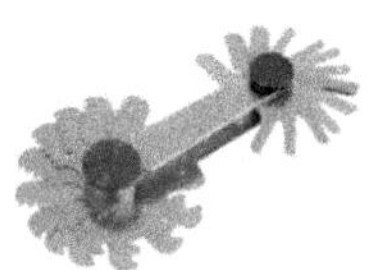

screw pitch gauge

Tap Die

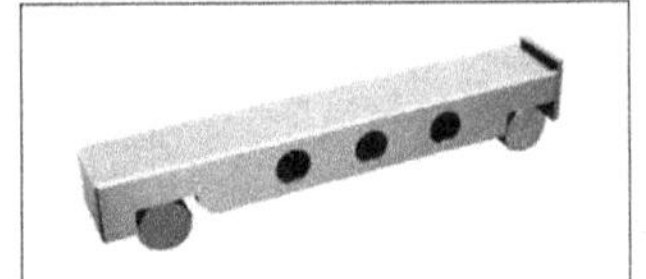

Sine bar

Slip gauge

Dial test indicator

Telescopic gauge

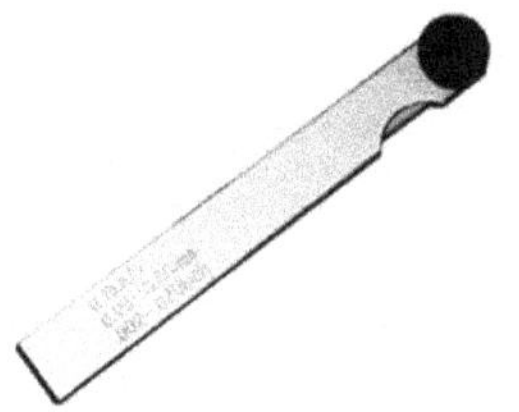

Feeler gauge

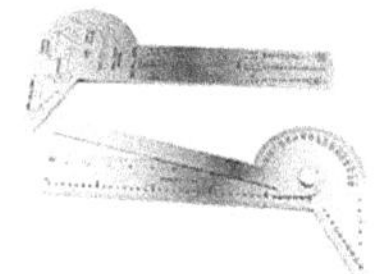

Centre gauge

Jig

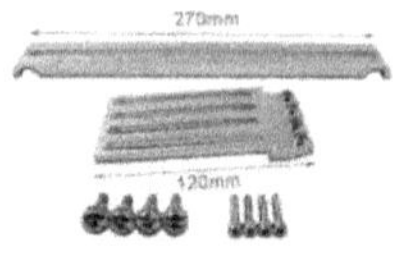

Fixture

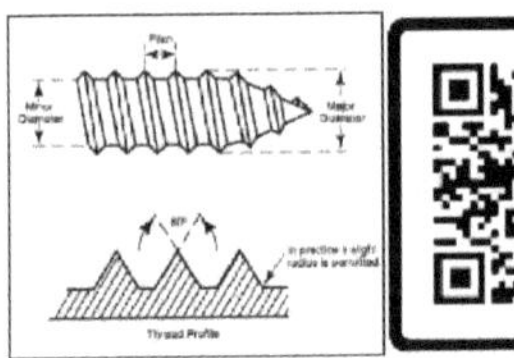

Thread

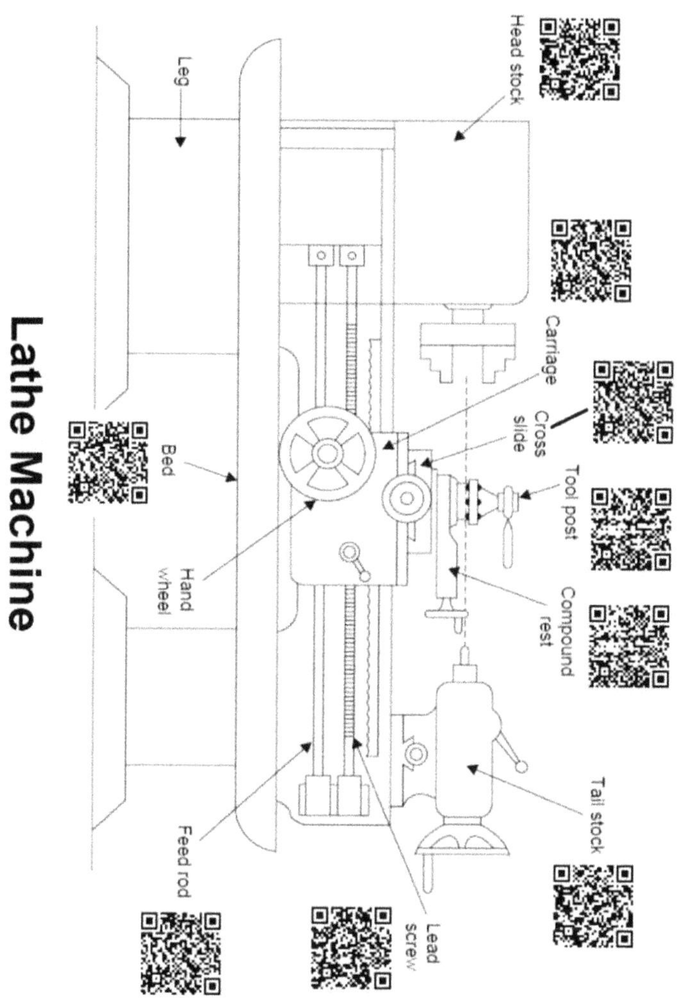
Lathe Machine
Head stock
Carriage
Cross slide
Tool post
Compound rest
Tail stock
Lead screw
Feed rod
Hand wheel
Bed
Leg

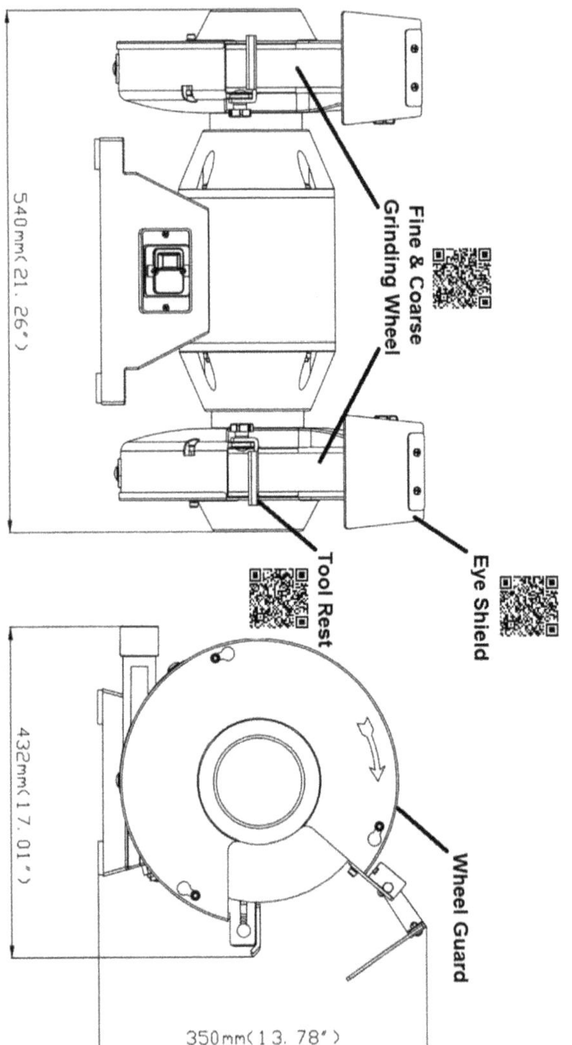
Bench Grinding Machine
Fine & Coarse
Grinding Wheel
Eye Shield
Tool Rest
Wheel Guard
540mm(21.26")
432mm(17.01")
350mm(13.78")

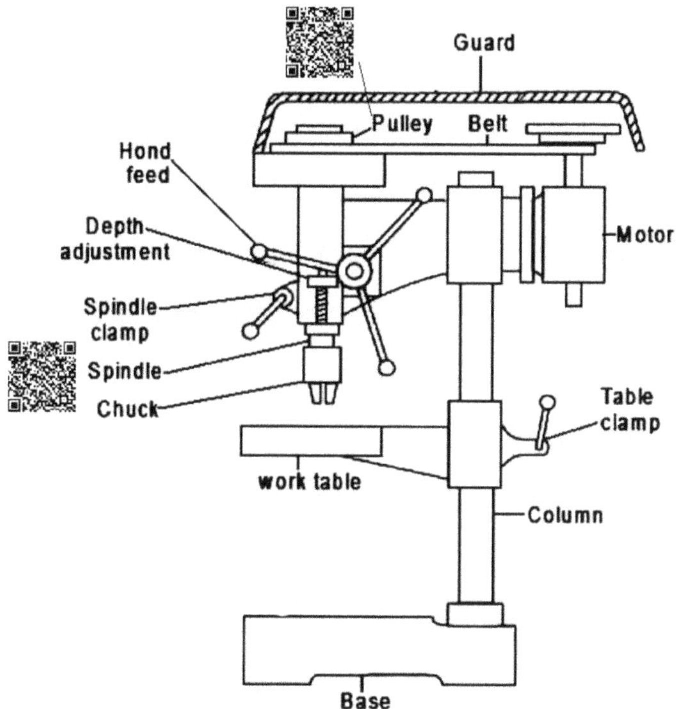

Piller Drilling Machine

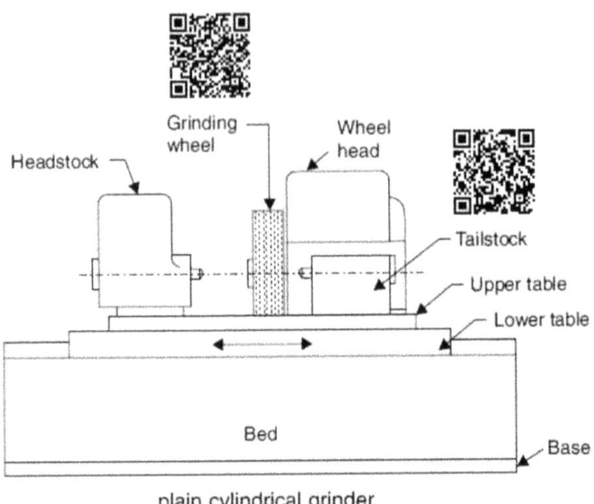

plain cylindrical grinder

Cylindrical grinding machine

To study Different operations and parts of Surface Grinding Machine

SURFACE GRINDER

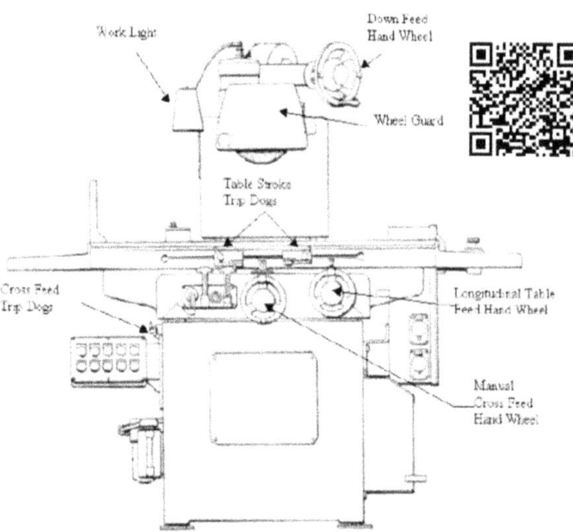

Surface grinding is used to produce a smooth finish on flat surfaces. It is a widely used abrasive machining process in which a spinning wheel covered in rough particles (grinding wheel) cuts

PLAIN OR HORIZONTAL MILLING MACHINE

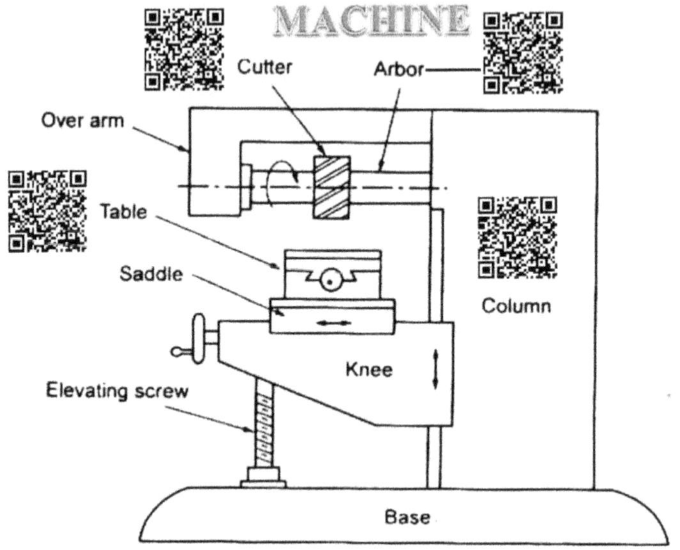

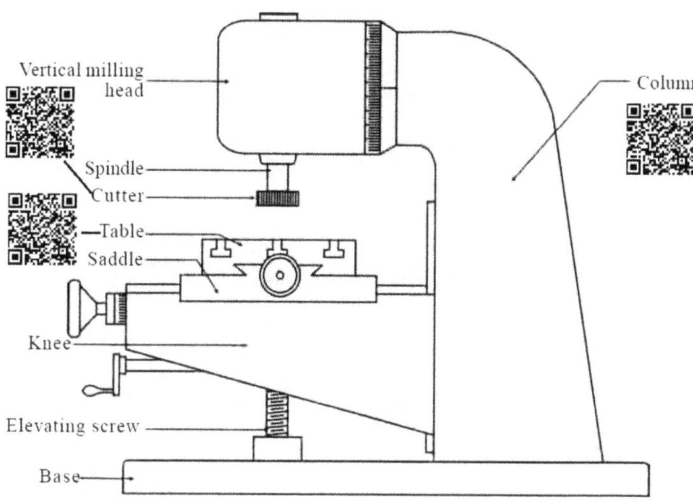

Vertical Milling Machine

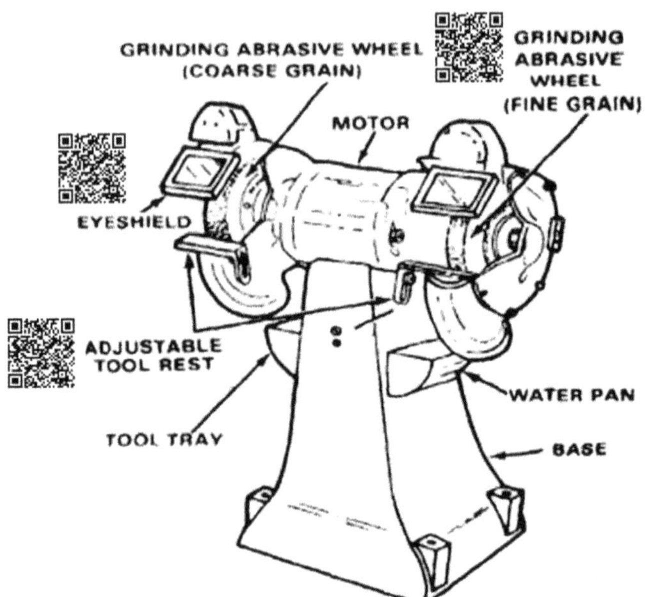

Pedastal Grinding Machine

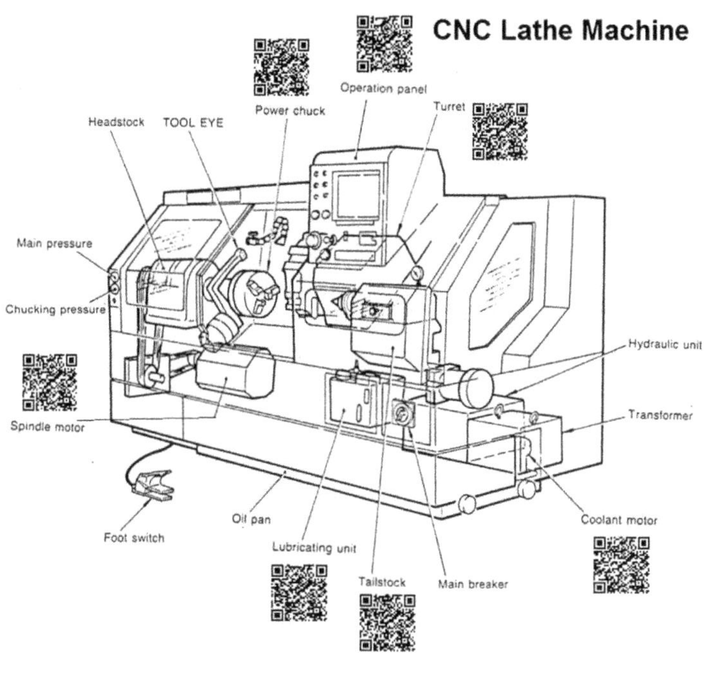
CNC Lathe Machine
Operation panel
Power chuck
Turret
Headstock
TOOL EYE
Main pressure
Chucking pressure
Hydraulic unit
Transformer
Spindle motor
Coolant motor
Oil pan
Foot switch
Lubricating unit
Tailstock
Main breaker

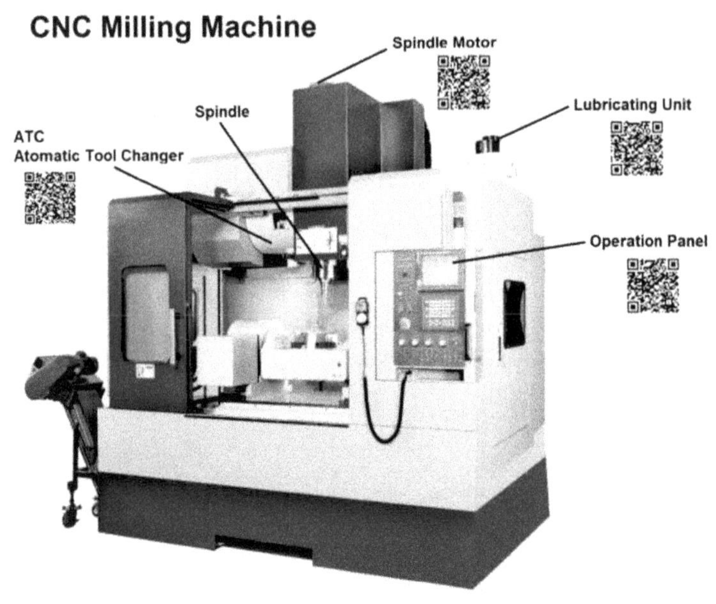

CNC Machine Power Pack

Tool Change & Spindle Speed in CNC Machine.

Coolant in CNC Machine.

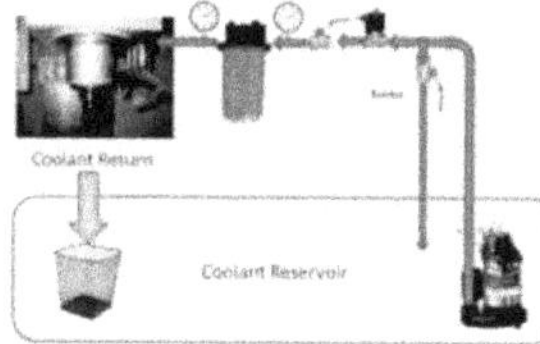

CHAPTER TWO

Machinist Grinder Second Year MCQ

01] To grind singular surface in two different planes of a job --------is used to hold

A] Plain vice

B] Universal vice

C] Magnetic

D] Face plate

02] The approach and over travel for surface grinding is ---------mm.

A] 5-10mm

B] 10-15mm

C] 7.5-12 mm

D] 12-17 mm

Hammers.png

03] While aligning the machine vice with reference to the table traverse a -------------hammer should use for striking.

A] Plastic hammer

B] Ball peen hammer

C] Wooden hammer

D] Rubber hammer

04] The magnetic chuck is aligned -----with the traverse of the work table

A] Perpendicular

B] Angular

C] Parallel

D] Parallel and perpendicular

05] Which of the following is precision grinding machine?

A] Pedestal grinding machine

C] Cylindrical surface and Tool & Cutter grinding machine

B] Bench grinding machine

D] Hand grinding machine

06] In grinding machine, how the table movement is reversed?

A] By limit switch

B] By proximities

C] By stoppers

D] By trip dogs

bench grinder-wheel.png

07] Which is not the property of hydraulic fluid used in grinding machine?

A] it must not control or absorb air

B] it must not cause corrosion of the moving parts

C] Should have adequate viscosity

D] it must vaporize at the operating temperature

(i] Pedestal Grinder

08] Pedestal grinding machine is held by ------------

A] Machine

B] Hand

C] Fixture

D] Table

09] The gap between the wheel face and tool rest should be ---

A] 4 mm

B] 5 mm

C] Zero

D] 3 mm

10]The equipment which removes residual magnetism from the ground work piece. .

A] De-magnetizer

B] Electromagnet

C] Permanent magnet

D] None of the above

11] Details to be given to specify a magnetic chuck ------

A] Types whether electromagnetic

B] Length of the chuck

C] Plain vice

D] All of these

12] in which type of grinding machine, the magnetic chuck are being used?

A] Surface grinding machine

B] Cylindrical grinding machine

C] Internal grinding machine

D] Cam shaft grinding machine

14] The most popular chuck on surface grinder is ----------

A] Pneumatic chuck

B] Hydraulic chuck

C] Magnetic chuck

D} Three law chuck

Lathe Chuck.png

15} The limitation of the magnetic chuck is---------

A] Variable holding pressure

B] Longer setup time

C] Difficulty in centring and working with small work piece

D] None of the above

16] The purpose of the demagnetiser, when using a magnetic chuck is to ----

A] Demagnetise the chuck only

C] Demagnetise both the chuck and workpiece

D] None of these

17] Job with narrow surface, which cannot be rigidly held direct magnetic chuck -----------

A] Plain vice

B] Universal vice

C] Angle plate with 'C' clamp

D] Magnetic chuck

18] in a universal swivelling vice how many separate swiveling movement is provided.

A] 2

B] 3

C] 4

D] 5

19] For grinding the angular surfaces which one of the following work holding device is preferred

A] Face plate

B] Four jaw chuck

C] Universal vice

D] Live centres

20] Name the grinding machine to grind round surface on rod.

A} Surface grinding machine

B] Tool & Cutter grinder

C] Cylindrical grinding machine

D] Cam shaft grinder

21] Name the cylindrical grinding machine part which moves perpendicular to the table movement.

A] Base

B] Head stock

C] Tail stock

D] Wheel head

22] Cylindrical grinder is ---------

A] Plain cylindrical grinder

B] Universal grinder

C] Centre less grinder

D] All of these

23] Plain cylindrical grinders can be used to produce—

A} Tapers

B] Under cut

C] Concave and convex radius

D] All of these

(v] Internal Grinder

24] How will you ensure the correctness of the internal radius?

A] By radius gauge

B] By seating a round ball bearing

C] By template

D] By grinding a internal to one equal to the radius of job to the operation

25] Name the grinding machine on which bore grinding is done.

A] Cylindrical grinder

B] Internal cylindrical grinder

C] Surface grinding

D] Centre less grinder

26] The face grinding is done in --------

A] Surface grinder

B] External cylindrical grinder

C] Internal cylindrical grinder

D] Camshaft grinder

27] Internal grinding machines are used to produce ----

A] Internal cylindrical holes

B] Tapered surface

C] Flat surface

D] None of these

28] TOOl and cutter are re-shaped by ------------

A] Surface grinding machine

B] tool and cutter grinding machine

C] Cylindrical grinding machine

D] Rotary grinding machine

29] Name the part of a tool and cutter grinder on which wheel head is being mounted.

A] Base

B] Saddle

C] Column

D] Table

32] The error due to faulty centre holes are eliminated by operation of -------

A] Surface grinder

B] centre-less grinder

C] Tool and cutter grinder

D] Cylindrical grinder

33] In centre less grinding, the work piece rest on -----

A] Centre of the chuck

B] Face plate

C] Rest blade

D] Ali of these

34] Which one of the following is not an advantage of centre grinding?

A] Easier handling of the woe piece during loading and unloading

B] Handling of the longer work pieces

C] Both shaft and brittle work piece could be handled

D] Low grinding speed

36] The value of one division on sleeve of a metric outside micrometer is?

A] 2.00mm

B] 1.00mm

C] 0.50mm

D] 1.50mm

Out Side Micrometer.png

37] Lock nut in micrometer is provided to ----------

A] Measure the job accurately

B] Lock the micrometer when it is not in use

C] Lock the reading after setting is over the job

D] Control the movement of the spindle

38} A micrometer has a positive error of 0.02mm. What is the correct reading when the micrometre measures 25.41mm?

A] 25.39mm

B] 25.39mm

C] 25.39mm

D] 25-39mm

Dial Guage.png

40] Which one of the following instruments is used to check the connectivity of the outside diameter?

A] Vernier calliper

B] Outside micrometer

C] Dial test indicator

D] Dial calliper

41] A micrometer has a positive error of 0.02 mm. What is the correct reading when the micrometer measures 25.41 mm?

A] 25.37 mm

B] 25.39 mm

C] 25.43 mm

D] 25.45 mm

42] in which one of the following micrometer the graduations on thimble and sleeve are in reverse direction to that of outside micrometer?

A] Inside micrometer

B] Depth micrometer

C] Tube micrometer

D] Flange micrometer

43] Micrometer works on the principle of ------

A] Screw

B] Bolt

C] Stud

D] Nut & Screw

(ii] Inside Micrometer -

44] The smallest inside micrometer has the graduation marked on the sleeve

A] 10mm

B] 12mm

C] 13mm

D] 25mm

Depth Micrometer.png

45] The graduations of a depth micrometer is ---------

A] in the reverse direction to that of the outside micrometer both thimble and sleeves

B] In the reverse direction only of the sleeve

C] In the reverse direction only on the thimble

D] Similar to an outside micrometer

46] The least count of a depth micrometer is -----------in metric system

A] 1mm

B] 0.001mm

C] 0.0001mm

D] 0.01mm

47] The pitch of the spindle of a depth micrometer is --------in metric pitch.

A] 0.01 mm

B] 0.02 mm

C] 0.3 mm

D] 0.5 mm

52] Which of the following is an indirect measuring tool?

A] Vernier calliper

B] Universal bevel protractor

C] Inside caliper

D} lnsrde micrometer

(vii] Vernier Caliper -

53] The minimum measurement that can be correctly read with a vernier caliper is called?

A] Least count

B] Zero reading

C] Main scale reading

D] Actual reading

Vernier Caliper 1.png

54] Least count of vernier Calliper is ----------

A] 1 M.S.D-1 V.S.D

B] 1 V.S.D-1 M.S.D

C] 2 M.S.D-1 V.S.D

D] 1 M.S.D+1 V.S.D

55] To check the width of (21H8] a -----------is used

A] Depth vernier

B] Outside micrometer

C] Vernier calliper

D] Dial Test Indicator

56] The minimum measurement that can be correctly read with a Vernier caliper is known as –

A] Zero reading

B] Least count

C] Main scale reading

D] Actual reading -Zero error

57] On which part of the vernier height gauge are the main scale division graduated? .

A] Base

B] Vernier plate

C] Beam

D] Fine adjusting unit

Vernier Height
Gauge.png

58] For marking purpose a Vernier height gauge must be on the --------

A] Bed of a machine tool

B] Surface plate

C] Square block

D] Any flat surface

59] Before using Vernier height gauge make sure that the --------

A] Locking screw is in a locked position

B] Scriber is Locked

C] Zero of the vernier coincides with zero of the main scale

D] Gib is Provided

60] The least count Of a vernier height gauge is............

A] 0.05 mm

B] 0.1 mm

C] 0.02 mm

D] 0001 mm

61] Which laying out the vernier height gauge must be used on the ----------

A] V block

B] Machine bed

C] Surface plate

D] Any flat surface

62] The part which is slides on the beam of a vernier height gauge is known as a ------

A] Base

B] Beam scale

C] Scriber

D] Vernier slide

63] The base of the vernier height gauge is generally made out of ---------

A] Cast iron.

B] Steel

C] Aluminium alloy

D] Tungsten carbide

64] Which instrument iis used for marking layout?

A] Micrometer

B] Vernier

C] Depth gauge

D] Vernier height gauge

65] While marking with a Vernier height gauge, the work piece is generally ----------

A] Supported by an angle plate

B] Supported by another work piece

C] Held by one hand

D] Held without support

Vernier Bevel
Protractor.png

66] The least count of vernier bevel protractor is?

A] 1 minute

<u>B] 5 minute</u>

C] 10 minute

D] 2‘3 minute

67] While measuring with vernier bevel protractor, which part is normally used as reference surface?

A] Blade

B] Dial

C] Disc

<u>D] Stock</u>

68] In Vernier bevel protractor is designed to measure?

A] Acute angles

B] Obtuse angles

<u>C] Acute and Obtuse angle</u>

D] Liner dimensions

69] On which part of the vernier bevel protractor are the main scale divisions graduated?

<u>A] Disc</u>

B] Blade

C] Dial

D] Stock

70] To get least count of 5 in a vernier bevel protractor the 23° main scale are divided into -..

A] 12 equal parts on vernier scale

B] 22 equal parts on vernier scale

C] 24 equal parts on vernier scale

D] 25 equal parts on vernier scale

73] Which of the following is not the part of a combination set?

A] Stock

B] Square head

C] Protractor head

D] Centre head

74} Uses of a dial test indicator are ----------

A] To check plane surface for parallelism and flatness

B] To check the straightness of shaft and bars

C] To check concentricity of holes and shafts

D] All the above

Dial Guage.png

75] The dial test indicators shows that the measurement as -------

A] The magnified small variation is size through a point

B] The difference between the top steps of the 5 mm

C] The actual size of the component

D] The direct reading of the dimension

76] Name the instrument which magnifies the small variation is size measured.

A] Vernier calliper

B] Micrometer

C] Dial indicator

D] Steel rule

77] Surface plates are made of............

A] High grade cast steel

B] Fine grained cast iron

C] Alloy steels

D] Wrought iron

79] The main use Of surface plate is for.................

A] Resting fixture

B] Lapping the component surface

C] Marking datum surface

D] Steel rule

(ii] 'V' Block & 'c' Clamp 04

80] A block level is used for checking

A] Only angular alignment

B] Vertical and Horizontal alignment

C] Only vertical alignment

D] Only horizontal alignment

V Block.png

81] To grind the flat surface on a cylindrical surface we use ---------
A] Universal vice
B] Magnetic chuck
<u>C] 'V' block with 'U' clamps</u>
D] Plain vice
82] To grind the face of a cylindrical work piece to 90° ------
A] Angle plate with 'C' clamp
B] Universal vice
C] Plain vice
<u>D] 'v' block with 'v' clamp</u>
83] The purpose of the v block is ------
A] Holding the flat surface
<u>B] Holding the cylindrical surface</u>
C] (A] & (B]
D] None of these
84] ------------- is used for grinding die steel and sharp edged tools
A] Silicon carbide
<u>B] Green silicon carbide</u>
C] Aluminium oxide

D] White aluminium oxide

85] -----is used for grinding carbide cutting tools

A] Green grit silicon carbide

B] Silicon carbide

C] White aluminium oxide

D] Aluminium oxide

86] Silicon carbide is ---------than aluminium oxide.

A] Softer

B] Harder

C] Smaller

D] Bigger

88] Which one is denoted by the letters Go?

A] Silicon carbide

B] White aluminium oxide

C] Green grits Silicon carbide

D] Aluminium oxide

89] ------------ is used for low tensile strength materials

A] Aluminium oxide

B] Green grit silicon carbide

C] Silicon carbide

D] White Aluminium oxide

bench grinder-wheel.png

90] ----------is used for grinding non-ferrous materials

A] Silicon carbide

B] Aluminium oxide

C] White Aluminium oxide

D] Green grit silicon carbide

91] Name the grinding wheel which perform the grinding fast and cool.

A] Aluminium oxide

B] Silicon carbide

C] Diamond

D] Cubic boron oxide

92] Which abrasive has the highest degree of hardness?

A] Corundum

B] Silicon carbide

C] Boron nitride

D] Diamond

(ii] Bond -05

93] The bond of a grinding wheel suitable for grinding of fine edged tool is.........

A] Shellac

B] Metal

C] Resinoid

D] Vitrified

94] it is denoted by the letter 'R' and is suitable for cutting off wheels

A] Vitrified bond

B] Silicate bond

C] Shellac bond

D] Rubber bond

95] it is denoted by the letter B and is used where rapid stock removal is necessary ---

A] Shellac bond

B] Rubber bond

C] Resinoid bond

D] Silicate bond

96] Usage of bond in grinding wheel is ------

A] To grind the work

B] To hold the material together

C] To from the grinding wheel shape

D] To hold the abrasive grains and to form the wheel shape

97] For HSS with vitrified bond preferred a cutting speed (m/min] in the range 0 -------

A] 5 to 10

B] 10 to 15

C] 15 to 20

D] 15 to 25

(iii] Grain -05

99] Grain is also known as ---------

A] Grade

B] Grit

C] Grip

D] Grape

101] given grit size of grinding wheel 46, select suitable grinding operation ----------

A] For pedestal grinding used for edge preparation in welder shop

B] For both roughing and finishing of hardened job on surface grinder

C] For roughing operation on surface grinder

D] To be used in cylindrical grinder

102] For grinding operation which grit size of grinding wheel is suitable for re sharpening the blunt single point tools on bench grinder finishing operation ----------

A] 36

B] 46

C] 60

D] 80

103] in grinding operation, for grinding softer materials --------

A] Coarser grain size is used

B] Fin grain size is used

C] Medium grain size is used

D] Any grain size may be used

(iv] Structure

104] Open structured wheel is used for ----------

A] Better cooling is required

B] High work speed

C] Rough finishing

D] Light and old machine

105] The structure of the grinding wheel depends upon --------

A] Hardness of the material being ground

B] Nature of the grinding operation

C] Finish required

D] All of these (v] Grade

106] Soft wheel is used when

A] The stock of material to be removed is heavier cut

B] High finish required

C] Area of contact is more

D] Grinding hard materials

107] me grade or grinding wheel depends on.................

A] Softness

B] Hardness

C] Brittleness

D] Porosity

108] ln grinding practice, the term hardness of the wheel or grade of the wheel" refers to --------

A] Hardness of the abrasives used

B] Strength of the bond of the wheel

C] Hardness of the work piece

D] Type of abrasive used

(vi] Types of Grinding Wheel 04

109] Standard shapes of a grinding wheel are designated by ----------

A] Types of number

B] Types of grains

C] Types of wheels

D] Types of shapes

110] Relict holes provided in the work piece are to accommodate the sharp -----------of the grinding wheel.

A] Corner

B] Middle

C] Cross

D] Parallel to face

111] while grinding the bottom surface of deep slot, the wheel ----------- should not rub the top surface of slot. .

A] Top

B] Side

C] Bottom

D] Front

112] Straight land surface is cut by tool and cutter grinder with-----------------

A] Plain wheel

B] Cup wheel

C] Conical wheel

D] Disc wheel

(vii] Specification of Grinding Wheel

113] Specification of a grinding wheel is 180x 13x 31.75 An 46/ 54-H8-VG what is the thickness of the grinding wheel.

A] 46/54

B] H8

C] 13

D] 31.75

114] Specification of grinding wheel 180 X 13 X 31.75 AA 46/54-H8 VG. What is the size of the abrasive grains?

A] 13

B] 31.75

C] H8

D] 46/54

115] How many characteristic symbols are in the grinding wheel standard marking?

A] 8 .

B] 7

C] 6

D] 5

116] A grinding wheel specification is given as 51-A-46-H-5-V-S in which number 46 stands for ----

A] Grade

B] Bond

C] Grain size

D] Structure

117] in specification of grinding wheel 51 A -46 -L 5 -V -23, A represent --------

A] Bond type

B] Abrasive type

C] Grain size

D] Bond grade

118, A grinding wheel is complete specified by the followmg elements take

A] Type of Abrasive, Grain size, Grade, Structure, Bond

B] Grain size, Grade, Structure, Type of Abrasive, Bond

C] Structure, Bond, Grain size, Type of Abrasive, Grade

D] None of the above

05] GRINDING WHEEL SELECTION 09

119] The stock of the material to be removed is more with heavy cut, we use --------

A] Soft wheel

B] Coarse grain open structure and hard grade wheel

C] Fine grain and dense structure

D] Soft grade and Coarse gram wheel

120} Fine grit, hard grade grinding wheel requires ----------grinding allowances than coarse soft grade wheels

A] Leis

B] More

C] Equal

D] None of the above

121] For grinding hard material ----------

A] Line grains and dense structure

B] Soft grade and coarse grain wheel

C] Soft wheel.
D] Coarse grain open structure and hard grade wheel
122] Soft grade and coarse grain wheel ---------
A] Low work speed
B] Area of contact is more select
C] For grinding hard materials
D] High finish requires
123] High finish requires -------
A] Soft grade and coarse grain wheel
B] Soft wheel
C] Fine grain and dense structure
D] Coarse grain open structure and hard grade wheel
124] Hard grade and dense structure wheel ----------
A] High wheel speed
B] Rough finish
C] For light and old machine
D] If better cooling is required
125] Rough finish -----------' the open structure
A] Open structured wheel
B] Coarse gram an
C] nags wheel
D] Hard grade and dense structure and structure wheel
128] What Should be the general grinding allowance for finishing?
A] 0.05 to 0.10 mm
B] 0.10 to 0.20 mm
C] 0.20 to 0.50 mm
D] 0.50 to 1 mm
(ii] Tolerance 01
129] Precision grinders are used to maintain close tolerance up to ---
A] 0.001 mm
B] 0.010 mm
C] 0.002 mm
D] 0.020 mm
130] The measuring stylus of a mechanical surface indicator is made of -------
A] Diamond
B] Tool steel
C] Carbide

D] Cast alloy

131] Name the geometrical test of mandrel shown in figure.

A] Check for ovality

B] Check for taper

C] Check for eccentric

D] Check for concentric

132] ISO 9000 pertains to ....

Productivity

B] Safety cleanliness

C] Cleanliness

D] Updating the records

133] The first spark should be pick up at -----

A] Right hand end of work

B] Left hand end work

C] The middle of work

D] The high spot of the work

134] Grinding wheel balancing is required for ------

A] Turning the wheel

B] To remove more material

C] Minimize the machine vibration during grinding

D] To run at higher speed

137] 'B' type centre is provided on mandrel is -----------------'

A] To engagement of centre support

B] To drive the mandrel

C] To protect the centre from damage

D] To reduce the weight 0 e

139] Collar type mandrels are used for checking of ------

A] Bore type component

B] Shaft type component

C] Bore with seating face component

D] Face seating component

140] Collets are made out of ----------

A] Mild steel

B] Tool steel

C] Spring steel

D] Construction steel

141] To expose new position to the grinding wheel, the diamond point should be turned to --form its previous position. 0

A] 60°

B] 90°

C] 45°

D] 30

142] If this operation is done frequently the wheel life becomes shorter d.

A] Glazing

B] Truing

C] Dressing

D] Loa mg

145] The process of equalizing the centrifugal force developed during grinding ---------

A] Glazing

B] Truing

C] Loading

D] Dressing

147] Grinding Wheel truing is the process for ----------------

A] Removing of clogs

B] Removing 0f run out.

C] Removing of glazing

D] Removing of out of balance

148] The pores of the wheel are clogged which chips ----------

A] Truing

B] Dressing

C] Glazing

D] Loading

149] Loss of sharpness and polished surface of a grinding wheel is known as -----

A] Loading

B] Dressing

C] Truing

D] Glazing

150] Reason for glazing of grinding wheel is-----

A] The wheel speed is too fast

B] The wheel speed is too slow

C] The grain size is too fine

D] All of these

151] A grinding wheel gets glazed due to --------

A] Wear of abrasive grains

B] Wear of bond

C] Cracks in wheel

D] Sharpening of wheel

152] Dry grinding requires --------grinding allowance than wet grinding.

A] Less

B] Equal

C] More

D] None of these

153] The advantage of wet grinder is ------------

A] Dust extractor requirement

B] Grinding wheel wears faster

C] Flying particle are spoil the atmosphere

D] Grinding operation able to control effectively

154] Purpose of using the coolant in grinding operation is ------

A] To reduce the heat of work

B] To reduce the heat of wheel

C] To reduce the heat of wheel and carry away the grinding dust

D] to maintain the machine temperature

155] water and paraffin mixed coolant is used for diamond wheel grinder the mixture ratio of coolant is......

A] 1:1

B] 1:2

C] 123

D] 1:4

156] What is the coolant mixing ratio of soluble oil and water to use on cast iron and hardened steel metals?

A] 1:20

B] 1:30

C] 1:40

D]1:60

157] Coolant retention is affected by the grinding wheel's --------

A] Hardness

B] Bond type

C] Grain size

D] Porosity

158] Which one of the following is not a property of cutting fluid?

A] Low specific heat

B] High lubricity

D] Chemical stability

C] High film boiling point

159] Extreme pressure additive (EPA] is mixed with cutting fluid for improving its power of.

A] Cooling

B] Lubrication

D] Production of the machined surface

C] Cleaning of cutting zone

160] The main purpose for using a lubricant in machine tools is to ------

A] Cool down the making parts

B] Prevent machine tool from heating

C] Wet the making parts for close contact

D] Minimize the friction between the making parts

161] Limit of Size means..................

A] maximum and minimum size

B] Maximum and maximum size

C] Maximum and middle size

D] Middle and minimum size

limit fit tolerance.png

162] As per standard, how many fundamental deviation are existing?

A] 23

B] 25

C] 27

D] 29

164] Interchange ability is normally applied for ------

A] Repairing of parts

B] Mass production

C] Single piece production

D] All of these

165] In hole basis system............

A] The size of the shaft is made constant

B] The size of the hole is made constant

C] The permissible tolerance are given on the hole and the shaft

D] Allowance is given only on the hole

166] The advantage obtained by giving tolerance on the hole is to ------

A] Increase the production

B] Decrease the production

C] Finish the component accurately

D] Produce the parts within the required permissible size error

167] A gear box shaft is fitted with bearing specified as 20 H7/g6. What is the type of fit?

A] Clearance fit

B] Transition fit

C] Interference fit

D] Heavy interference fit

168] The difference between maximum limit of size to its corresponding basic size of a component is»

A] Actual deviation

B] Upper Deviation

C] Tolerance

D] Lower limit

169] A Name the gauge used for quick measurement of a diameter and thickness.

A] Limit gauge

B] Ring gauge

C] Plug gauge

D] Snap gauge

170] Which one of the following is not the function of a taper gauge?

A] Measurement of groove and gap

B] To measure the hole size

C] To measure the slot width

D] To find the surface finish

171] A plug gauge which has its "Go" and "No Go" size on the same end is known as --------

A] Single ended plug gauge

B] Double ended plug gauge

C] Progressive plug gauge

D] Continuous plug gauge

172] "Go" side of plug gauge will have the diameter equal to ~~~~~~

A] ACRE

B] Maximum size of the job

C] Basic size of the job

D] Maximum size of the job

173] In a taper plug gauge the Go and No Go ends sizes are denoted by a step on ------

A] Separately

B] The both sides

C] The same side

D] The either side

174] A function of the plug gauge is to ------

A] Measure the outer diameter of the work piece

B] Measure the length of the work piece

C] Measure the internal diameter of the hole

D] Measure the angle of the surface (ii] Plain Ring Gauge 01

175] A plain ring gauge is used for checking.............

A] Taper holes

B] External diameter of cylindrical parts

C] Internal diameter of cylindrical parts

D] Major diameter of external thread

Slip Gauge.png

176] Slip gauges are meant for............
A] Coarse measurement
C] Accurate measurement
B] Fine measurement
D] Critical measurement
177] Filler gauge is used to measure ------
A] Accurate measurement
B] Fine measurement
C] Radial distance
D] Gap
178] Function of the filler gauge is to ------
A] Measure the diameter of the specimen
B] Measure gap width
C] Measure the height of specimen
D] Measure the curvature
179] The internal radius is turned in outer race of ball bearing. .
A] For eight bit
B] For all circulation
C] For bail seating in bearing
D] For matching convenience

180] Calculate Grinding is the process of removing material by a ---------- action.

<u>A] Rubbing</u>

B] Cutting

C] Polishing

D] Wearing

181] Which one of the following methods of application is not preferred for grinding process?

A] Liquid jet

<u>C] Intermittent supply</u>

B] Flood under gravity

D] Mixed with compressed air

183] The recommended depth of cut for roughing is -----------

A] 0.020 to 0.040mm

B] 0.015 to 0.050mm

C] 0.010 to 0.020mm

<u>D] 0.015 to 0.030mm</u>

184] Preferred depth of cut for surface grinding during finishing operation is in the range----

A] 0.5 to 1 mm

B] 0.05 to 1 mm

<u>C] 0.005 to 0.01 mm</u>

D] 0.0005 to 0.01 mm

185] Crack is developed in grinding wheel due to ....

A] Generation of heat

<u>B] High speed</u>

C] Slower speed

D] None of these

186] The distance moved by the wheel across the work surface per stroke is referred to as 1.....

A] Depth of cut

<u>B] Feed</u>

C] Cutting speed

D] Heavy cut

187] Calculate surface speed of grinding wheel having spindle speed 1000 rpm and the diameter of wheel 350mm

<u>A] 18.31m/sec</u>

B] 18.3m/min

C] 18.31mm/ rev

D] lam/sec

188] calculate the spindle speed of a grinding machine having surface speed of 50meterl sec and the diameter of wheel is 300mm

A] 3814mm

B] 3184mm

C] 4184mm

D] 4814mm

190] The grinding wheel speed is expressed in ----------

A] Meter/ Revolution

B] Meter/Second

C] Meter/ Minute

D] mm/Revolution

191] Calculate surface speed of grinding wheel having spindle speed of 2000 rpm and the diameter of wheel 300 mm.

A] 30.4 m/sec

B] 33 m/sec

C] 31.4 ml sec

D] 31 m/m

192] Calculate the spindle speed of grinding machine having surface speed of 30 meter/ sec and the diameter of wheel is 200 mm.

A] 9554 rpm

B] 8554 rpm

C] 9455 rpm

D] Silicate bond

194] For a grinding wheel diameter of 300mm runs with a speed of 942 m/min, then the R.P.M. is given by ....

A] 1000

B] 500

C] 800

D] 10000

(iv] Travers Feed -

195] The correct rate of table traverse for finish grinding is ---------

A] 1/3 of wheel width / revolution of work

B] 2/3 of wheel width / revolution of work

C] Equal to wheel width / revolution of work

D] 1/2 of wheel width / revolution of work

196] Feed in grinding depends on --------

A] Width-of wheel

B] Finish required

C] Power of machine

D] Both la] 8103]

197] Maximum feed fort rough grinding is given by -----------. .

A] 0.9 times the face width of grinding wheel

B] 0.5 times the face Width of the grinding wheel

C] 1.2 times of the width of the grinding wheel

D] 2 times of the grinding width of the gr. wheel

198] The R.P.M. of the grinding wheel for internal grinding are high as compared to that of external grinding because ....

A] Peripheral speed for internal grinding are high

B] Grinding wheels are small

C] Arc of contact of works 'with the wheel is greater

D] Grinding allowance is high

199] Calculate the rpm of the grinding wheel for the given data of cylindrical grinder, where D = 300m, n = 3.14, CS = 1600.

A] 1625 rpm

B] 1650 rpm

C] 1700 rpm

D] 1750 rpm

200] The process of embedding the abrasive on lapping called ---

A] Fixing

B] Rubbing

C] Charging

D] Lapping

201] Which one of the following is the advantage of pneumatic system?

A] For low cost layout

B] For increasing the rate of production

C] For better working environment

D] All of these

202] CNC lathe has in-built co-ordinates measuring system. The Zero position of this coordinate system is called

A] Reference point

C] Work zero point

B] Machine Zero point

D] Programme zero point

203] While measuring zero offset in CNC machine shouid be in

A] MDI mode

B] Jog mode

C] Automatic mode

D] Preset mode

204] Command 'M' will order the machine to perform an operation. 'M' command will perform operation at the beginning or at the end of the cycle. Command M03 means ---

A] End of programme and reset.

B] Clockwise rotation of spinde

C] Stopping the programme

D] End the programme

205] Which one. of the following is not the feature of a CNC machine?

B] Coolant supply

A] Automatic tool changer

D] Ball screws

C] Servomotor

206] Which one of the following is not correct statement about CNC machine?

A] Continuous operation.

B] Can be updated by using new software

C] Can machine complex shapes

D] Only highly skilled worker can work

207] Which one of the following represents the classification of CNC systems?

A] Point to point or Continuous system

B] Incremental or Absolute system

C] Open loop or Closed loop system

D] All of these

208] The purpose of the activity log is used to find -------------,

A] The unproductive time

B] Time spend on each activity

C] Whether the most important work is done at prescribed time or not

D] All of these

209] Which one of the following are incorporated in cycle, time?

A] Process time

B] Delay time

C] Transportation time

D] All of these

210] Contouring controls are ---------------

A] Open loop systems

B] Close-loop systems

C] Both (A] & (B]

D] None of these

02] GRINDING MACHING 06

211] Part of machine .... used to produce rigidity to the machine and support's all other parts.

A] Head stock

B] Tail stock

C] Base

D] Work table

212] -----------A part of machine IS used to produces rigidity to the madame and supports all other parts. . . .

A] Head stock

B] Tail stock

C] Base .

D]Work table

213] Which one are the precision grinder?

A] Surface grinder

B] Cylindrical grinder

C] Tool and cutter grinders

D] All of these

214] Which One is the type of precision grinder?

A] Surface grinder

B] Cylindrical grinder

C] Tool and cutter grinders.

D] All of these

215] How the grinding machines are specified? Hine

A] By Size of work piece that can be mounted on the machine

B] By using number of instrument

C] Fixing of safety guards

D] Weight of machine

216] The function of wheel head is............

A] It carries the grinding wheel

B] It carries motor

C] It carries the grinding wheel and motor

D] It carries the spindle

(i] Surface grinder O4

217] For production of finishing of flat and plane surface on a work piece the method of grinding employed is............

A] External cylindrical grinding

B] Internal cylindrical grinding

C] Surface grinding '

D] Universal type tool grinding

218] For roughing operation-on surface grinder, which one is suitable size grinding wheel ?

A] 36 grit size of grinding wheel

B] 46 grit size of grinding wheel

C] 60 grit size of grinding wheel

D] 80 grit size of grinding wheel

219] In which grinding machine is used to machine plane or flat surface / stepped surfaces

A] Surface

B] Tool and Cutter

C] Centre less I

D] Bench

220] In grinding irregular, curved, tapered, convex and concave surfaces, the grinder used is ~

A] Cylindrical grinder

B] Internal grinder

C] Surface grinder

D] Tool & Cutter grinder .

(ii] Holding devices of surface grinder A. Magnetic chuck 06

221] Magnetic chuck is used for holding, the --------~

A] Cooper work piece

B] Steel work piece

C] Aluminium work piece

D] Brass work piece

222] How non-magnetic materials are held on magnetic chucks?

A] By clamping them with a suitable steel fixture

B] By clamping in machine vice

C] By clamping a C-Clamp

D] By clamping in catch plate

223] Types of magnets Used in Magnetic includes --------'

A] Electra magnets

B] Permanent magnets

C]‘ Both electro and permanent ‘magnets

D] No magnets are used

(iii] Cylindrical grinder 04

224] In cylindrical grinders, work is held in ---------

A] Magnetic chucks

B] Regulating wheel

C] Supporting wheel

D] Between centres

225] The method of grinding used to produce a straight or tapered surface on a work piece, is

A] Internal cylindrical grinding

B] Form grinding

C] External cylindrical grinding

D] Surface grinding

226] ln transverse grinders ---------

A] The work is reciprocated as the wheel feeds to produce cylinders longer than the width of wheel face

B] The work rotates in a fixed position as the wheel feeds to produce cylinders equal to or shorter than the width of wheel face

C] The work is reciprocated as the wheel feeds to produce cylinders shorter than the width of wheel face

D] The work rotates in a fixed position as the wheel feeds to produce cylinders longer than the width of wheel face

227] Which process is used for grinding splinted shafts? .

A] External cylindrical grinding

B] Internal cylindrical grinding.

C] Surface grinding.

D] Form grinding

228] For holding the work piece which has already bored, the work holding device used Is ---

A] V block

B] Tailstock

C] Mandrel

D] Vice

229] For a short work piece, work holding devices Is -----------

A] TWO Jaw chuck and three Jaw chuck.

B] Four law chuck and Pneumatic chuck

C] Magnetic chuck.

D] All of these

230] What are the uses of internal grinders? .

A] To produce straight work pieces

B] To produce Formed holes on work pieces

C] To produce tapered work pieces

D] All the above.

231] Which one of the types is an internal grinder?

A] Chucking grinders

B] Planetary grinders

C] Centre less grinders

D] All the above

232] ------grinder is used for only work pieces which can be held in a chuck.

A] Chucking

B] Planetary

C] Centre less

D] Bench

233] ---------grinder lS used for jobs which cannot be held and rotated in a chuck.

A] Chucking.

B] Planetary

C] Centre less

D] Bench

234] The method of grinding used to produce internal cylindrical holes and tapers, is—

A] Internal cylindrical grinding

B] Form grinding

C] External cylindrical grinding

D] Surface grinding

(v] Tool and cutter grinder

235] Which type of grinding machine Is used for sharpening of tool is milling cutters/drills/hobs/broaches?

A] Chucking.

B] Tool and cutter

C] Centre less

D] Bench

236] Which type of grinding machine Is used for sharpening of miilingtools?

A] Chucking.

B] Tool and cutter

C] Centre less

D] Bench

237] Thread grinding requires work speed ------------.

A] Fast

B] Medium

C] Very low

D] Low

238] Thread grinders is a ----------

A] Bench grinding machine

B] Pedestal grinder machine

C] Precision grinder machine

D] Special grinding machine

239] Thread grinding requires work speed from ------.

A] 1 to 3 m/min

B] 5 to 10 m/min

C] 10 to 14 m/min

D] 14 to 20 WW“

(vii] Roll grinder -‘02

240] Roll grinders are ---------.

A] Larger.

b] Much larger

C] Smaller

D] Medium size

(viii] Centre less grinder

241] ---------Grinder is used to grind exterior cylindrical/tapered/ formed surfaces

A] Chucking

B] Planetary

C] Centre less

D] Bench

242] Which one are the main elements of centre less grinder?

A] Grinding wheel

B] Regulating-wheel

C] Work rest

D] All of these

243] In Centre grinding the components used include.

A] Regulating wheel

B] Grinding wheel

C] Work rest

D] All of these

244] In Centre less grinding the speed of the regulating wheel is ------------

A] Equal to the speed of the Grinding wheel

B] More than the speed of the Grinding wheel

C] Lesser than the speed of the Grinding wheel

D] All of these

245] Internal Centre less Grinding Process is -----------

A] Completely Manual work

B] Partially Automatic

C] Fully automatic

D] Will vary with size of the component

246] The advantage of Centre less Grinding Includes-um---

A] Shorter Loading time

B] Lesser operation time

D] All of these

247] The conditions under which work is heled between the centres include.

A] When the centre have already one end

B] When the centre.

C] When the work is already bored and has no

D] All of these

248] The method of centre less grinding used to produce taper is ---------

A] In-feed grinding.

B] Through feed grinding

C] End feed grinding

D] All of these

249] Which machine can be used for grinding the ball bearing outer races?

A] Cylindrical grinding machine '

B] Centre less grinding machine

C] Surface grinding machine

D] Universal grinding machine

250] ------------ is user! for grinding crankshaft of Automobile engines I Air craft engines I compressors etc. .

A] Crank shaft grinder

B] Tool post grinder

C] Thread grinder

D] Surface grinder

251] ------------ is Used for grinding crankshaft of Automobile engines / Aircraft.

A] Crank shaft grinder

B] Tool post grinder

C] Thread grinder

D] Surface grinder

(x] Piston grinder

252] ---------is used for grinding piston of high speed internal combustion engines.

A] Crank Shaft grinder

B] Tool post grinder

C] Thread grinder

D] Piston grinder

253] Piston grinders is used to--------

A] Automobile engines.

B] Generate threads for cylindrical grinding

C] High speed internal combustion engines

D] Lathe centres

254] The function of the Bevel Protractor is to

A] Measure the angle

B] Set the work holding devices on machine tool or work table

C] Both (a] & (b]

D] None of these

(ii] Dial Test Indicator (D.T.l.]

255] Which one of the following is not correct about dial test indicator?

A] It has 100 divisions on its dial

B] Motion of the stem is transferred to the dial through Gear train

C] Its accuracy is 0.1 mm

D] Used in conjunction with depth gauge

(Ii i]Slip gauge20

256] A slip gauge is a ----------

A] Rectangular block

B] Square block

C] Cubic block

D] Cylindrical block

257] In 4th SERIES of slip gauge, which one of the following range is correct in set 46 pieces

A] 1.0 to 9.0 mm.

B] 1.001 101.009 mm

C] 1.01 to 1.09 mm

D]'1.1'to_-1.9mm

258] In 5th SERIES of slip gauge, which one Of the following range is correct in set 46 pieces –

A] 100to 100 mm '

B] 1.001 to 1.009 mm

C] 1.01 to 0.09mrn

D] 11 to 9mm

259] In 2NDS SERIES of slip gauge, which one of the following range IS correct in set of 45 pieces-

A] 1.0 to 9.0 mm

B] 1.001 to 1. 009 mm

C] 1.01 to 1.09 mm

D] 1.1 to 1.9mm

260] In 3RD SERIES of slip gauge, which one of the following range is correct in set 46 pieces –

A] 10.0 to 100 mm

B] 1.001 to 1.009 mm

C] 1.01 to 1.09 mm

D] 1.1 to 1.9 mm

261] In 1ST SERIES of slip gauge, which one of the following range is correct in set 46 pieces –

A] 0.001mm

B] 001mm

C] 0.1mm

D] 1.0mm

262] In 2ned SERIES of slip gauge, which one of the following STEP is correct in set of 46 pieces –

A] 0.001mm

B] 0.01 mm

C] 0.1 mm

D] 1-0 mm

263] In 3rd SERIES of slip gauge, which one of the following STEP Is correct in set 46 pieces

A] 0.001mm

B] 0.01mm

C] 0.1 mm

D] 1.0mm

264] Size of the Gauge block In the 4th Series of M 112 type are in the range of--------

A] 25 mm to 100 mm

B] 10 mm to 25 mm

C] 0.5 mm to 24.5 mm

D] 0.5 mm to 100 mm

265] Which one of the following Grades of slip gauges is used for calibration purpose only?

A] Grade 01

B] Grade 00

C] Grade 0.

D] Grade 02

266] Which one of the following chemicals is used for cleaning the Gauge Blocks?

A] Sodium chloride.

B] Carbon Tetrachloride

C] Potassium dichromate

D] Potassium chloride

(iv] Sine Bar

267] which one of the following statement about Sine bar is not correct?

A] Uses tow precision rollers kept on either side

B] Made of the Chromium steel

C] The surface is lapped

D] The centrelines of the holes will be inclined to the top surface

268] determine the angle of taper, when a sine bar of 200mm length is used for measuring the slip block of height 100mm.

A] 45°

B] 60°

C] 30°

269] A sin bar is available In standard sizes. Which one of the following Is NOT a standard size of the sin bar?

A] 100mm
B] 200mm
C] 250mm
D] 3oomm
270] The Productivity depends upon---------------
A]Design of the product and Process
B] Operation of the process
C] Quality of equipment
D] All of these
271] Which one of the following is not the part of the Job Card?
A] Component or product
B] Quantity to be manufactured
C] Details of the coolant
D] Manufacturing Schedule
05] JIGS 8. FIXTURES
272] Purpose of the Box Jig is to
A] Hold the job and guide the tool to produce internal threads
B] To produce many inclined holes
C] To produce many straight holes
D] None of these
273] Jigs and fixtures are --------.
A] Machining tools
B] Precision tools
C] Both (a] & (b]
D] None of these
274] 'How jig are in terms of weight compared to fixtures?
A] Jigs are lighter than fixtures
B] Jigs are heavier than fixtures
C] jigs are equal in weight to fixtures for same operation
D] None of these
275] Which fixtures are used for machining parts which musthav-e machined details evenw spaced?
A] Profile fixtures
B] Duplex fixtures
C] Indexing fixtures
D] None of these
276] In this process in order to keep the stone clean and sharp, it is necessary to use coolant ----'

A] Lapping
B] Honing
C] Burnishing
D] Super finishing

277] --------is used to maintain close tolerance When using Precision grinders.

A] 0.001 mm
B] 0.010 mm
C] 0. 002 mm
D] 0 020 mm

278] In order to obtain a surface finish in the range of 0.75 PM to 1.25 urn, the operation used is called ---

A] Grinding .
B] Lopping
C] Honing
D] Buffing

Lapping

279] This process is carried out using fine abrasive materials------------------

A] Super finishing
B] Honing.
C] Burnishing
D] Lapping

280] In this process the compound used COnsists of Silicon carbide, aluminium oxide, boron, carbide and diamond

A] Honing
B] Super finishing
C] Lapping
D] Burnishing

281] Lapping pressure for hard materials is approximate equal to --------

A] 1 WWW
B] 0.5 N/mm
C] 0.2 N/mm
D] 0.7 N/mm

(ii] Honing

282] This process is carried out in both hardened and unhardened state ------

A] Burnishing

B] Super finishing

C] Lapping

D] Honing

283] Honing process is preferred for -------------.

A] Finishing internal holes

B] Boring of carbides

C] Internal threads cutting '

D] External grinding

284] The range of surface roughness in Honing is in the range of --------

A] 0.9 to 5 microns

B] 0.1 to 5 microns

C] 0.13 to 1.25 microns

D] 0 to 100 microns

285] Which of the followings are examplcs of honing operation'?

A] Roller bearing races

B] Diesel engine cylinder bore

C] Hub holes in gears boxes.

D] All of these.

286] The productivity of honing Operation is

A] Less than the productivity of lapping Operation

B] More than the productivity of lapping operation

C] Equal to the productivity of lapping operation for the same work piece

D] None of these

(iii] Burnishing

287] This process is consists of moving a very hard surface over work piece to remove irregularities -------

A] Lapping

B] Honing

C] Burnishing

D] Super finishing

O7] MACHINIST 08

288] The maximum size (diameter] of cutter that can be ground using a face milling attachment?

A] 200 mm diameter

B] 300 mm diameter

C] 400 mm diameter '

D] 500 mm diameter

289] What Is the size of the adopter. supplied with the tilting head of radius grinding attachment for holding end mills?

A] No.5 Brown and sharp taper adopter

B] No.6 Brown and sharp taper adopter

C]. No.7 Brown and sharp taper adopter

<u>D] No.8 Brown and sharp taper adopter</u>

290] The action 0f grinding wheel is similar to that of milling cutter ---------

A] Compare grinding wheel with abrasive wheel

<u>B] Compare grinding wheel with milling cutter</u>

C] Compare grinding wheel with reamer

D] Compare grinding wheel with lathe cutting tool

291] For re-sharpening of milling cutter in tool and cutter grinder, which one is suitable size grinding wheel?

A] .35 grit size of grinding wheel

B] 46 grit size of grinding wheel

<u>C] 60 grit size of grinding wheel</u>

D] 80 grit size of grinding wheel

292] Slitting saw can be sharpened with -------

<u>A] Universal tool and cutter grinder</u>

B] Diamond tool

C] Surface grinder

D] Abrasive stick

293] The purpose of secondary clearance angle in milling cutter is ---------------

A] To increase primary clearance.

<u>B] To reduce land width to nominal width</u>

C] To increase land width

D] To reduce primary clearance

294] For cutting a straight land ----------

<u>A] A cup type grinding wheel is used.</u>

B] A tapered type grinding wheel is used

C] A surface grinding wheel is used

D] External grinding.

295] for high speed parting off work on material like cemented carbide Is‘

A] Do all machine

B] Cutting off machine

C] Heavy duty power saw

D] Mining machine sitting saw

296] Which one of the following statements is true with reference to the tool life?

A] Time between starting and finishing a job

B] Total time for turning work including regrinding

C] Time between two successive regrinds

D] Time between starting of metal cutting and too\ wear out

297] Which one of the following tool angle is provided to avoid rubbing of body of the tool with the work piece?

A] Rake angle

B] Helix angle

C] Clearance angle

D] None of these

09] GRINDING DEFECT & CAUSES 06

298] Which one are common faults occur with the grinding wheeP. _ .

A] Glazing

B] Loading

C] Gumming

D] All of these

299] The reason for quick wear out Of grinding wheel is -------

A] Soft wheel

B] Improper transverse work speed

C] Very low speed of the grinding wheel than recommended

D] All of these

300] The reason for having scratches on the surface of the work piece subsequent to grinding operation is -------‘

A] Grains are very coarse I

B] Dirty coolant

C] Both dirty coolant and coarse grain size

D] Very fine grain size

301] A very hard wheel with high wheel speed produces which of the following defects?

A] Scratch

B] Poor finish

C] Surface of the work piece gets cracks

D] The grinding wheel gets cracked

302] Work out of roundness is due to --------- .

A] Work out of balance.

B] Worn bearings

C] Work springing due to excessive pressure

D] All of these

303] The cause of the Tapered bore include ---------

A] Bell mouthing

B] Wheel not allowed sparking

C] Work head misalignment

D] All of these '

10] WHEEL LODING & GLAZING

304] Glazing Is the -----------------

A] Wheel has lost its sharpnes$ and has a polished surface

B] Process of the wheel is equalizing the centrifugal developed during grinding.

C] Pores of the wheel are clogged with chips

D] If this operation is done frequently the Wheel life becomes shorter

305] Reason for glazing of grinding Wheel is______________

A] The wheel speed is too fast.

B] The wheel speed is too low

C] The grain size is coarse.

D] The grain size is medium

306] Reason for glazing of grinding wheel is ---------

A] The wheel speed is too medium fast

B] The wheel speed is slow

C] The grain size is Coarse I '

D] The grain size is too tine

307] Glazing in grinding wheels can be decreased by ------

A] Using a harder wheel or by increasing the wheel speed

B] Using a softer wheel or by decreasing the wheel speed

C] Using a harder wheel or by decreasing the wheel speed

D] Using a softer wheel or by increasing the wheel speed

308] It is commonly observed that the face of a grinding wheel becomes shiny and smooth or glazed after some use due to one of the following reasons

A] Grade of wheel is too hard .

B] Abrasive of wheel is not suitable for the purpose

C] Grain size is too coarse

D] Structure of the wheel is too open

11] WHEEL DRESSING 81 Truing

309] Truing is -----------------

A] The wheel has lost its sharpness and has a polished surface

B] If this operation is done frequently the wheel life becomes shorter

C] The process of equalizing the centrifugal force developed during grinding

D] All the above

310] ---------is the Operation of re-sharpening of grinding whee.

A] Truing

B] Dressing

C] Aligning

D] Brazing

311] Removing blunt abrasive particles from the wheel is known as --------

A] Truing

B] Dressing

C] Loading

D] Glazing

312] Dressing IS the ---------

A] The wheel has lost its sharpness and has a polished surface

B] The process of equalizing the centrifugal force developed during grinding

C] The wheel has lost its sharpness and has a polished surface

D] If this Operation is done frequently the wheel life becomes shorter

313] Abrasive sticks are used for dressing ------------

A] Very thin Wheels

B] For cutter grinders

C] Both (A & B]

D] None of these

12] WHEEL BALANCING 01

314] Grinding wheels should be tested for balance -------------.

A] Only at the time of manufacture

B] Before starting the grinding operation

C] At the end of grinding operation.

D] Occasionally

13] GRINDING WHEEL SELECTION 10

315] For light and old machine -------------

A] High finish requires

B] Soft grade and coarse grain wheel
C] Hard grade and dense structure wheel
D] Grinding hard material
316] Fine grain and dense structure (wheel -------------
A] High finish requires
B] Soft grade and coarse grain wheel
C] Hard grade and dense structure wheel
D] Grinding hard material
317] Coarse grains/ softer wheel is used for -------
A] Small area of contact
B] Lower work speed
C] Larger area of contact
D] Higher work speed
318] Finer grains] harder wheel is used for -------
A] Small area of contact
B] Lower work speed
C] Larger area of contact
D] Higher work speed
319] Which are the constant factors for selecting a grinding wheel?
A] Material to be ground
B] Type of grinding machines
C] Amount stock to be removed
D] All of these
320] Area Of Contact is more select ----------
A] High finish requires
B] Soft grade and coarse grain wheel
C] Hard grade and dense structure wheel
D] Grinding hard material
321] Soft wheel ------------
A] High finish requires
B] Soft grade and coarse grain wheel
C] Hard grade and dense structure wheel
D] Grinding hard material
322] The high spot of the work, while starting grinding operation «m
A] First spark pick up
B] Second spark pick up
C] No spark pick up
D] Third spark pick up

323] Harder grinding wheel is used for.............
A] Small area of contact
B] Lower work speed
C] Larger area of contact
D] Higher work speeds.
324] Softer grinding wheels is used for ------
A] Small area of contact.
B] Lower work speed
C] Larger area of contact
D] Higher work speed
325] Green grits silicon carbide is denoted by the letters ---------
A] A
B] c
C] B
D] G
326] The artificial abrasive is............
A] Emery
B] Aluminium oxide
C] Diamond
D] 0M3
327] In which grinding wheel is used for grind carbide tools ---------
A] Aluminium oxide
B] Silicon carbide
C] Diamond.
D] Green silicon carbide
328] Diamond is used for -------------
A] Machining hard surfaces.
B] Precision grinding
C] Dresser for Precision wheels
D] All of these
329] The abrasive recommended for grinding materials of high tensile strength is ------
A] Silicon carbide
B] Aluminium oxide
C] Sand stone
D] Diamond
330] The aluminium oxide abrasive is chiefly used for grinding -----------
A] High speed steel

B] Carbon steel.

C] Wrought iron.

D] All of these

331] For faster cutting, wheel used on a cutting off machine Is ------

A] Metal bond wheel

B] BResinoid bond wheel

C] Rubber bond wheel.

D] Shellac bond wheel

332] ----------------is used to hold the abrasive particles together to the required size to form the grinding wheels.

A] Bond

B] Structure

C] Grains

D] Abrasive

333] It Is the substance, mixed with abrasive grains to hold them together

A] Bond

B] Coolant

C] Lubrication

D] Lubricant

334] in which bond Is used for grinding cams and rolls requiring high finish ----

A] Resinoid bond

B] Vitrified bond

C] Shellac bond

D] Rubber bond

335] -------------bond IS suitable for high rate of stock removal.

A] Vitrified bond wheels

B] Resinoid bond wheels

C] Shellac bond wheels.

D] Rubber bond wheels

336] What grit size of grinding wheels is suitable for re-sharpening the blunt single point tool on bench grinder finishing operation?

A] 36

B] 46

C] 60

D] 80

337] A coarse grained grinding wheel is used to grind -------------

A] Hard and brittle materials

B] Soft and ductile materials

C] Hard and ductile materials

D] Soft and brittle materials

338] 1 n which processes the material is remove due to the action of abrasive grains?

A] Electro-Chemical Grinding (ECG]

B] Ultrasonic Machining lUSM]

C] Laser Beam Machining (LBM]

D] Electrical Discharge Machining lEDM]

339] As per Indian Standards the grain size '280' comes under the group --

A] Coarse

B] Medium

C] Fine.

D] Very Fine

340] How the grinding wheels are graded? . .

A] Soft ('A' to 'H']

B] Medium ('I' to 'P']

C] Hard ('O.' to 'Z']

D] All of these

341] The hardness Of a grinding wheel IS specified by -------------

A] Brielle hardness number

B] Rock well hardness number

C] Vickers pyramid number

D] Letter of alphabet

342] The structure of a grinding wheel depends Upon ------- -----

A] Hardness of the material being ground

B] Nature of the grinding operation

C] Finish required

D] All of these

343] A dense structure of a grinding Wheel Is used for --------

A] Hard materials

B] Brittle materials

C] Finishing cuts

D] All of these

344] Which of the following processes remove maximum amount of material out of a work piece?

A] Honing

B] Lapping

C] Grinding

D] Super finishing

345] What is use of traverse grinding?

A] It is used to grind work pieces longer than the width of the wheel face .

B] It is used to grind work pieces smaller than the width of the wheel face

C] It is used to grind work pieces equal to width of the wheel face

D] It is used to grind work pieces shorter than the width of the Wheel lace

346] What is use of traverse grinding?

A] It is used to grind work pieces longer than the width of the whee] face

B] It is used to grind Work pieces smaller than the width of the wheel face

C] It is used to grind of work pieces equal to width of the wheel face

D] None of these

347] The grinding fluid should have --------

A] High viscosity

B] Low hush point

C] Coerciveness

D] High heat absorption

348] A mixture of paraffin and water coolant is recommended for -------

A] Grinding

B] Lapping cemented carbide.

C] Diamond wheel

D] Grinding or lapping cemented carbide with diamond wheel

349] HOW the grinding Wheel should be operated?

A] Dry grinding

B] Wet grinding

C] Hard grinding

D] Soft grinding

350] Advantage of using cutting fluid during grinding operation is ------

A] 5000 surface finish

B] Reduction in cutting forces

C] Reduction in hardening of the work piece

D] All of these.

351] Which one of the following statements is correct about Straight oi\ s is correct?

A] Good lubricant and Poor coolant.

B] Good lubricant and Good coolant

C] Poor lubricant and Poor coolant

D] Poor lubricant and Good coolant

352] Which one of the following are the coolant used during Grinding?

A] Chemical fluids

B] Semi chemical

C] Emulsions

D] All of these

353] 0.015 to 0.030 mm depth of cut is recommended for --------

A] Finish

B] Rough

C] Semi finish

D] Super finish

354] While mounting a new grinding wheel on a grinder, the test used to find out the damage of the wheel?

A] A sound test by tapping the wheel with a non-metallic object

B] A sound test by using a steel hammer

C] Rolling test by allowing the wheel to roll on the floor

D] A test runs with a very high surface speed

355] Visual inspection Of the grinding wheel is done to ---------

A] Broken or chipped edges.

B] Cracks on the surface of the wheel

C] Damaged mounting bushing.

D] All of these

356] A cracked wheel, when beaten with a mallet gives ---------.

A] Clear sound

B] Dull sound.

C] No sound

D] None of these

cnc lathe qr.jpg

cnc milling machine.jpg

CNC Machine Tape Punch

image

357] Tape punch having 1 inch in width tape it is made by

A] Paper Mylar

B] Aluminum Mylar

C] Plastic

D] Above all

358] In point two point positioning positioning system........] Is acceptable

A] Open loop control system

B] Closed loop control system

C] Above both

D] None of them

359] In CNC machine having.......

A] Lead screw

B] Ball lead screw

C] Above both

D] None of both

CNC Program Coordinate

image

360] The aim of sub program is........

A] For find coordinates X Y Z.

B] For other small machine.

C] To avoid cutting tool nose tool nose penetration in Jobs surface of high speed.

D] While machining of job in special condition do not use time to time of program block.

361] What is mean by while while xyz co-ordinate point measure zero-measurement

A] Reference mark.

B] Work zero

C] Co-ordinate points

D] Above all

362] CNC machine specified by axis......

A] 2 axis

B] 3 axis

C] 4 axis

D] Above all

CNC Machine Axis

image

363] Xyz axis of CNC machines which point is used for measurements.

A] Work zero point

B] Machine zero point

C] Common zero point

D] Above all

364] Following which point is not useful in CNC machine.

A] various operation done on CNC machine.

B] Less amount for inspection.

C] Hard for setting measure.

D] Machine efficiency is depend upon operators skill.

365] For selection of zero offset before necessary..........

A] cutter is fixed on machine table.

B] The data entered in machine.

C] Job is fixed on machine table.

D] Speed and feed selection necessary before machine operates.

CNC Work Zero Offset Setting.

image

366] In zero offset program indicates........] Code of following

A] X y z

B] X0 y0 z00

C] X10 Y20 Z30

D] G71

367] Work zero is

A] Datum of machine zero on job position.

B] Indicate by X0Y0Z0.

C] Selection of point on job according to program.

D] The end of machining point

368] M command is used for starting operation and complete revolution cycle M03 means.

A] Stop the program.

B] Program completed and reset.

C] Complete the program.

D] Spindle clockwise motion.

CNC Machine Power Pack

image cnc lubricating-unit.png

369] CNC machine is not manually operated it is control by...........

A] Program

B] operation

C] Cam

D] Plug board system

370] In CNC machine M13 means

A] coolant stop

B] coolant on

C] spindle stop

D] coolant on & spindle on

371] The function of power pack in CNC machine.

A] For balancing of lubricants heat.

B] For increasing heat of lubricants.

C] For destroy heat of lubricant.

D] Above all.

CNC Machine Bed.

image

372] The section of CNC machine bed is.....

A] Flat

B] Half round

C] Rectangular

D] Triangular

373] Following which statement is disadvantage of CNC machine.

A] Less inspection charge.

B] Less tooling charge.

C] Increase production rate.

D] High establishment charge.

374] The point to point system is more effective for......

A] Turning

B] Profile milling

C] Grinding

D] Drilling

Tool Setting on NC Machine.

image

375] Tool setting on NC machine on......] unit.

A] Presetting device.

B] Order special device without machine.

C] On n c machine other empty time.

D] When other operation working on machine.

376] For measuring system having built-in coordinates in this system..........] is called zero position.

A] Reference point.

B] Machine zero point.

C] Work zero point

D] Program zero point.

377] Job turning on CNC machine 50 mm dia turn with programs said the trial run 50.1 mm at production time following which Idea used for correct dia making

A] by increase offset of tool 0.1 mm.

B] by increase offset of tool 0.05 mm

C] by decrease offset of tool 0.05 mm

D] by decrease offset of tool 0.1 mm

CNC Copying Lathe Machine.

image

378] For measure zero offset dim dimensions on CNC machine.........mode is set

A] MDI

B] Jog

C] Automatic

D] prcsct

379] Coping unit of copying lathe is work on

A] Mechanical power system

B] Hand power system

C] Hydraulic power system

D] None of them

380] Following which advantage of Pneumatic power system

A] For increase production rate.

B] Less cash for layout

C] Good climate for work

D] Above all

Principle of CNC Machine Templates.

image

381] For face copying........] Type template is used

A] Rounded

B] Plate type

C] Flat

D] Triangular

382]............] Is Main principle of CNC MACHINE?

A] Indicate all states in numbers

B] More time required for mechanical control on machine.

C] Cutting speed is more than manual control.

D] Production sequence in workshop is stored by block number in machine.

383] For copy of one shaft.......] Type template is used.

A] Rounded

B] Triangular

C] Flats

D] Square

CNC Program Tool Path.

image

384] The symptoms of continuous path is

A] Called counting system.

B] Tool and work piece on co-ordinate Axis for inter related motion.

C] By the setting of cutter feed and speed

D] Above all

385] Misc command M30 means........

A] End of program and reset

B] Program stop

C] Clockwise motion of spindle

D] Complete the programs

386] Following which affect on milling surface while by milling with unsetting spindle vertical milling machine with- longitudinal feed.

A] Convex surface

B] Concave surface

C] Radius cross line

D] Rough surface

CNC Milling Operation]

image

387] While milling by vertical milling machine with 12 mm dia end mill cutter through slot provide on mild steel plate the cutter is sleep and broken for this fault how it is avoid.

A] High speed spindle

B] Low cutting speed

C] Increase of cut depth

D] Less the depth and feed of cutter

388] Having 5 mm pitch of screw and dividing ratio of 40 : 1 what is lead of milling machine

A] 0.25 mm

B] 5 mm

C] 8 mm

D] 200 mm

389] If not use of backlash Eliminator slap cutter used for down milling operation which safety to be observed?

A] Less lead and depth

B] High lead

C] high lead and less depth

D] High lead and high speed

CNC Machine Zero & Feed Rate.

cnc machine zero.PNG

390] Zero offset is the distance between.....] And.........

A] G41 & g42

<u>B] Machine zero & work zero</u>

C] Reference point and tapping mode

D] None of them

391] The feed rate is programmed as mm per minute with G ....] And mm per- Revolution with G.

A] G41 & g42

B] G 43 and G 40

<u>C] G 94 and g95</u>

D] None of them

392] For collection all instructions from.......] In CNC control unit

<u>A] Memory</u>

B] Tape reader

C] Control panel

D] Operator

<u>CNC Drilling Machine.</u>

cnc drilling machine.jpg

393] For control forward and backward of- CNC drilling machine y axis.........

A] Spindle

B] Table

C] Clockwise

<u>D] Column</u>

394] M 01 command means.....

A] For stopping programs

B] End of program and reset

<u>C] Stopping programs condition</u>

D] Clockwise rotation of machine spindle

395] CNC machine is founded by American scientist john person in.......] Year

A] 1950

B] 1952

C] 1955

D] 1957

CNC Control, Input & Memory Unit.

cnc control.jpg

396] Name of unit used to command the CNC machine.

A] Control unit

B] Memory unit

C] Input unit

D] Output unit

397] Name of unit used to processing the data in CNC machine.

A] Memory unit

B] Control unit

C] Input unit

D] Output unit

398] Name of unit used to storing the data in CNC machine.

A] Input unit

B] Control unit

C] Memory unit

D] Output unit

Servo Motor in CNC Machine.

servo motor.jpg cnc spindle-motor.png

399] Name of unit used to calculation of data in CNC machine.

A] Output unit

B] Arithmetic unit

C] Memory unit

D] Input unit

400] Name of unit used to display result of processing data in CNC machine

A] Arithmetic unit

B] Output unit

C] Memory unit

D] Input unit

401] Servo Motor in CNC machine is used to.............

A] Changing tool on machine spindle

B] Driving machine spindle

C] Fixing job on machine spindle

D] Proving job on spindle

Types of CNC Machine.

types of cnc.jpg

402] One of the below part of CNC machine used to changing tools on spindle.

A] Servo Motor

B] Control panel

C] Automatic tool changer A T C

D] High speed spindle

403] One of the below CNC machine in CNC milling category is.......

A] Chucking centre

B] CNC late

C] Vertical machining centre

D] Surface grinding machine

404] One of the below CNC machine in turning centre or CNC lathe category is.......

A] Vertical machining centre

B] Horizontal machining centre

C] Vertical turning centre

D] Profile grinding machine

Miscellaneous Functions for CNC Machine.

miscellaneous function.jpg

405] One of the below CNC machine in grinding Centre category is.....

A] Universal milling centre

B] Cylindrical grinding machine

C] CNC late

D] Vertical machining centre

Grinding wheels 1 bench grinder-wheel.png

Grinding

406] In CNC Machine programming word M indicates

A] Feed rate

B] Spindle speed

C] Miscellaneous function

D] Tool number

407] In CNC Machine programming preparatory function G00 is for.....

A] Linear interpolation

B] Clockwise circular interpolation

C] Counter clockwise circular interpellation

D] Hold

Preparatory Functions for CNC Machine.

preparatory function.jpg

408] In CNC Machine programming preparatory function G02 is for.....

A] Linear interpolation

B] Clockwise circular interpolation

C] Counter clockwise circular interpellation

D] Hold

409] One of the bellow preparatory function G 00 is used in CNC program for.........

A] Linear interpellation or feed motion in straight line.

B] Clockwise circular interpellation

C] Point to point Positioning or Rapid motion.

D] Counter clockwise circular interpellation

410] One of the bellow preparatory function used in CNC program for 3D interpellation

A] G 05

B] G12

C] G17

D] G18

Threading & Tapping on CNC Machine.

threading & tapping on cnc.jpg

411] One of the bellow preparatory you function used in CNC program for thread cutting constant lead

A] G33

B] G40

C] G53

D] G62

412] One of the bellow preparatory function used in CNC program for tapping operation.

A] G-40

B] G53

C] G62

D] G63

413] One of the below preparatory function used in CNC program for milling operation.

A] G62

B] G63

C] G 78, 79

D] G81

Drilling, Boring & Reaming on CNC Machine

drilling boring & reaming.jpg

414] One of the bellow preparatory function used in CNC program for drilling operation.

A] G 81

B] G 82

C] G 84

D] G 85

415] One of the bellow preparatory function used in CNC program for reaming operation.

A] G 84

B] G 85

C] G 86

D] G 90

416] One of the below preparatory function used in CNC program for boring operation.

A] G 86

B] G 90

C] G 91

D] G 92

CNC Program Sequence Number.

cnc program sequence.png

417] In CNC program which letter is used to indicate the sequence number of the block

A] N

B] G

C] F

D] S

418] In CNC program which letter is used to indicate position of linear axis

A] ABC

B] UVW

C] XYZ

D] IJK

419] One of the below letters used in CNC program for Feed rate

A] S

B] F

C] T

D] M

Tool Change & Spindle Speed in CNC Machine.

tool change i cnc.jpg cnc milling atcautomatic-tool-changer-atc.png

420] One of the below letters used in CNC program for spindle speed in RPM

A] M

B] T

C] S

D] F

421] In CNC program which letter is used to indicate TOOL function number of tool

A] T

B] S

C] M

D] F

422] In CNC program which miscellaneous function used to program stop

A] M03

B] M00

C] M01

D] M02

CNC Machine Spindle Direction.

cnc machine spindle direction.png

423] One of the below miscellaneous function used to program optional Stop

A] M 01

B] M 02

C] M 03

D] M 04

424] In CNC program miscellaneous function M02 is used to......

A] Program stop

B] Optional program stop

C] End of program

D] Clockwise spindle on

425] In CNC program miscellaneous function M03 is used to..........

A] Counter clockwise spindle on

B] Clockwise spindle on

C] Spindle off

D] Tool change

Coolant in CNC Machine.

coolant in cnc machine.jpg

cnc coolant-pump.png

426] One of the below miscellaneous function used in CNC program for spindle stop.

A] M04
B] M05
C] M06
D] M07

427] In CNC program which miscellaneous function is used for Tools change

A] M06
B] M07
C] M09
D] M10

428] One of the below miscellaneous function used in CNC program for coolant on

A] M08
B] M09
C] M10
D] M11

Clamping the Job on CNC Machine.

clamping the job on cnc.jpg

429] One of the below miscellaneous function in CNC program used for coolant off

A] M11
B] M10
C] M9
D] M15

430] In CNC program which miscellaneous function used for clamping the job on machine table.

A] M09
B] M10
C] M11
D] M15

431] One of the below miscellaneous function in CNC program used for unclamp the job

A] M11

B] M15

C] M30

D] M60

Work piece change in CNC Machine.

workpice change in cnc.jpg

432] In CNC program which miscellaneous function used for change of workpiece

A] M30

B] M60

C] M68

D] M78

433] The machine is.........for zero off-setting on CNC Machine.

A] In MDI Mode

B] In JOG Mode

C] In Automatic Mode

D] In Present Mode

434] The feed rate on NC Machine is indicate by ......code.

A] X

B] Y

C] F

D] Z

CNC Machine Axis Position]

cnc machine axis position.jpg

435] The position of axis is indicate by.......code.

A] X,Y,Z

B] P,Q,R

C] A,B,C

D] M,N,O

436] CNC Drilling Machine is on.......Axis Programmed.

A] Two Axis

B] Three Axis

C] Four Axis

D] Six Axis

437] From.......unit collect instruction in control unit of CNC

A] Machine Tool

B] Instruction

C] Magnetic Box

D] Memory

Working Graph of CNC Machine]

working graph of cnc machine.jpg

438] For preparing tape of NC Machine----------code is used.

A] EIA Code

B] ISO Code

C] ASC Code

D] None of them.

439] CNC Machine gives more accurate production than convention machine, But it is more expensive because.

A] It has AC cabin

B] It has dust proof cabin

C] It has strong foundation

D] It has more space

440] CNC Machine is working on graphical base the point on digital line, indicated digital points call..........

A] Graph

B] Input Media

C] Co-Ordinate

D] Original Point

Axis Rotary Motion in CNC Machine]

axis rotary motion in CNC.png

441] On CNC Machine for longitudinal feed has.......axes, cross feed......axis and for vertical feed........axis name given.

A] A,B,C

B] X,Y,Z

C] P,Q,R

D] M,N,O

442] For rotary motion CNC machine axis has.......name given.

A] A,B,C

B] X,Y,Z

C] P,Q,R

D] M,N,O

443] CNC Machine means.......

A] Natural Control Machine

B] Pneumatic control Machine

C] Numerical Control Machine

D] No Command Machine

INDUSTRIAL TRAINING INSTITUTE

Monthly Test-1, Marks- 20, Date:- ______________

(Every Question Carry Two Marks)

1-06] In grinding machine, how the table movement is reversed?

A] By limit switch

B] By proximities

C] By stoppers

D] By trip dogs

2-07] Which is not the property of hydraulic fluid used in grinding machine?

A] it must not control or absorb air

B] it must not cause corrosion of the moving parts

C] Should have adequate viscosity

D] it must vaporize at the operating temperature

3-08] Pedestal grinding machine is held by -----------

A] Machine

B] Hand

C] Fixture

D] Table

4-09] The gap between the wheel face and tool rest should be ---

A] 4 mm

B] 5 mm

C] Zero

D] 3 mm

5-10]The equipment which removes residual magnetism from the ground work piece. .

A] De-magnetizer

B] Electromagnet

C] Permanent magnet

D] None of the above

6-11] Details to be given to specify a magnetic chuck ------

A] Types whether electromagnetic

B] Length of the chuck

C] Plain vice

D] All of these

7-12] in which type of grinding machine, the magnetic chuck are being used?

A] Surface grinding machine

B] Cylindrical grinding machine

C] Internal grinding machine

D] Cam shaft grinding machine

8-14] The most popular chuck on surface grinder is ----------

A] Pneumatic chuck

B] Hydraulic chuck

C] Magnetic chuck

D} Three law chuck

9-15} The limitation of the magnetic chuck is---------

A] Variable holding pressure

B] Longer setup time

C] Difficulty in centring and working with small work piece

D] None of the above

10-17] Job with narrow surface, which cannot be rigidly held direct magnetic chuck -----------

A] Plain vice

B] Universal vice

C] Angle plate with 'C' clamp

D] Magnetic chuck

INDUSTRIAL TRAINING INSTITUTE

Monthly Test-2, Marks- 20, Date:- _______________

(Every Question Carry Two Marks)

1-21] Name the cylindrical grinding machine part which moves perpendicular to the table

movement.

A] Base

B] Head stock

C] Tail stock

D] Wheel head

2-22] Cylindrical grinder is ---------

A] Plain cylindrical grinder

B] Universal grinder

C] Centre less grinder

D] All of these

3-23] Plain cylindrical grinders can be used to produce—

A} Tapers

B] Under cut

C] Concave and convex radius

D] All of these

4-24] How will you ensure the correctness of the internal radius?

A] By radius gauge

B] By seating a round ball bearing

C] By template

D] By grinding a internal to one equal to the radius of job to the operation

5-25] Name the grinding machine on which bore grinding is done.

A] Cylindrical grinder

B] Internal cylindrical grinder

C] Surface grinding

D] Centre less grinder

6-26] The face grinding is done in --------

A] Surface grinder

B] External cylindrical grinder

C] Internal cylindrical grinder

D] Camshaft grinder

7-27] Internal grinding machines are used to produce ----

A] Internal cylindrical holes

B] Tapered surface

C] Flat surface

D] None of these

8-28] TOOl and cutter are re-shaped by ------------

A] Surface grinding machine

B] tool and cutter grinding machine

C] Cylindrical grinding machine

D] Rotary grinding machine

9-29] Name the part of a tool and cutter grinder on which wheel head is being mounted.

A] Base

B] Saddle

C] Column

D] Table

10-32] The error due to faulty centre holes are eliminated by operation of -------

A] Surface grinder

B] centre-less grinder

C] Tool and cutter grinder

D] Cylindrical grinder

INDUSTRIAL TRAINING INSTITUTE

Monthly Test-3, Marks- 20, Date:- ______________

(Every Question Carry Two Marks)

1-36] The value of one division on sleeve of a metric outside micrometer is?

A] 2.00mm

B] 1.00mm

C] 0.50mm

D] 1.50mm

2-37] Lock nut in micrometer is provided to ----------

A] Measure the job accurately

B] Lock the micrometer when it is not in use

C] Lock the reading after setting is over the job

D] Control the movement of the spindle

3-38} A micrometer has a positive error of 0.02mm. What is the correct reading when the

micrometre measures 25.41mm?

A] 25.39mm

B] 25.39mm

C] 25.39mm

D] 25-39mm

4-40] Which one of the following instruments is used to check the connectivity of the outside

diameter?

A] Vernier calliper

B] Outside micrometer

C] Dial test indicator

D] Dial calliper

5-41] A micrometer has a positive error of 0.02 mm. What is the correct reading when the

micrometer measures 25.41 mm?

A] 25.37 mm

B] 25.39 mm

C] 25.43 mm

D] 25.45 mm

6-42] in which one of the following micrometer the graduations on thimble and sleeve are in

reverse direction to that of outside micrometer?

A] Inside micrometer

B] Depth micrometer

C] Tube micrometer

D] Flange micrometer

7-43] Micrometer works on the principle of ------

A] Screw

B] Bolt

C] Stud

D] Nut & Screw

8-44] The smallest inside micrometer has the graduation marked on the sleeve

A] 10mm

B] 12mm

C] 13mm

D] 25mm

9-45] The graduations of a depth micrometer is ---------

A] in the reverse direction to that of the outside micrometer both thimble and sleeves

B] In the reverse direction only of the sleeve

C] In the reverse direction only on the thimble

D] Similar to an outside micrometer

10-46] The least count of a depth micrometer is -----------in metric system

A] 1mm

B] 0.001mm

C] 0.0001mm

D] 0.01mm

INDUSTRIAL TRAINING INSTITUTE

Monthly Test-4, Marks- 20, Date:- _______________

(Every Question Carry Two Marks)

1-56] The minimum measurement that can be correctly read with a Vernier caliper is known as –

A] Zero reading
B] Least count
C] Main scale reading
D] Actual reading -Zero error

2-57] On which part of the vernier height gauge are the main scale division graduated? .

A] Base
B] Vernier plate
C] Beam
D] Fine adjusting unit

3-58] For marking purpose a Vernier height gauge must be on the --------

A] Bed of a machine tool
B] Surface plate
C] Square block
D] Any flat surface

4-59] Before using Vernier height gauge make sure that the --------

A] Locking screw is in a locked position
B] Scriber is Locked
C] Zero of the vernier coincides with zero of the main scale
D] Gib is Provided

5-60] The least count Of a vernier height gauge is............

A] 0.05 mm
B] 0.1 mm
C] 0.02 mm
D] 0001 mm

6-61] Which laying out the vernier height gauge must be used on the ----------

A] V block
B] Machine bed
C] Surface plate
D] Any flat surface

7-62] The part which is slides on the beam of a vernier height gauge is known as a ------

A] Base
B] Beam scale
C] Scriber
D] Vernier slide

8-63] The base of the vernier height gauge is generally made out of ---------

A] Cast iron.
B] Steel
C] Aluminium alloy
D] Tungsten carbide

9-64] Which instrument iis used for marking layout?
A] Micrometer
B] Vernier
C] Depth gauge
D] Vernier height gauge

10-65] While marking with a Vernier height gauge, the work piece is generally ----------
A] Supported by an angle plate
B] Supported by another work piece
C] Held by one hand
D] Held without support

INDUSTRIAL TRAINING INSTITUTE

Monthly Test-5, Marks- 20, Date:- _______________

(Every Question Carry Two Marks)

1-73] Which of the following is not the part of a combination set?
A] Stock
B] Square head
C] Protractor head
D] Centre head

2-74} Uses of a dial test indicator are ----------
A] To check plane surface for parallelism and flatness
B] To check the straightness of shaft and bars
C] To check concentricity of holes and shafts
D] All the above

3-75] The dial test indicators shows that the measurement as -------
A] The magnified small variation is size through a point
B] The difference between the top steps of the 5 mm
C] The actual size of the component
D] The direct reading of the dimension

4-76] Name the instrument which magnifies the small variation is size measured.
A] Vernier calliper

B] Micrometer
C] Dial indicator
D] Steel rule
5-77] Surface plates are made of............
A] High grade cast steel
B] Fine grained cast iron
C] Alloy steels
D] Wrought iron
6-79] The main use Of surface plate is for..................
A] Resting fixture
B] Lapping the component surface
C] Marking datum surface
D] Steel rule
7-80] A block level is used for checking
A] Only angular alignment
B] Vertical and Horizontal alignment
C] Only vertical alignment
D] Only horizontal alignment
8-81] To grind the flat surface on a cylindrical surface we use ---------
A] Universal vice
B] Magnetic chuck
C] 'V' block with 'U' clamps
D] Plain vice
9-82] To grind the face of a cylindrical work piece to 90° ------
A] Angle plate with 'C' clamp
B] Universal vice
C] Plain vice
D] 'v' block with 'v' clamp
10-83] The purpose of the v block is ------
A] Holding the flat surface
B] Holding the cylindrical surface
C] (A] & (B]
D] None of these

INDUSTRIAL TRAINING INSTITUTE
Monthly Test-6, Marks- 20, Date:- _______________
(Every Question Carry Two Marks)

1-86] Silicon carbide is ---------than aluminium oxide.
A] Softer

B] Harder

C] Smaller

D] Bigger

2-88] Which one is denoted by the letters Go?

A] Silicon carbide

B] White aluminium oxide

C] Green grits Silicon carbide

D] Aluminium oxide

3-89] ------------ is used for low tensile strength materials

A] Aluminium oxide

B] Green grit silicon carbide

C] Silicon carbide

D] White Aluminium oxide

4-90] ----------is used for grinding non-ferrous materials

A] Silicon carbide

B] Aluminium oxide

C] White Aluminium oxide

D] Green grit silicon carbide

5-91] Name the grinding wheel which perform the grinding fast and cool.

A] Aluminium oxide

B] Silicon carbide

C] Diamond

D] Cubic boron oxide

6-92] Which abrasive has the highest degree of hardness?

A] Corundum

B] Silicon carbide

C] Boron nitride

D] Diamond

7-93] The bond of a grinding wheel suitable for grinding of fine edged tool is.........

A] Shellac

B] Metal

C] Resinoid

D] Vitrified

8-94] it is denoted by the letter 'R' and is suitable for cutting off wheels

A] Vitrified bond

B] Silicate bond

C] Shellac bond

D] Rubber bond

9-95] it is denoted by the letter B and is used where rapid stock removal is necessary ---

A] Shellac bond

B] Rubber bond

C] Resinoid bond

D] Silicate bond

10-96] Usage of bond in grinding wheel is ------

A] To grind the work

B] To hold the material together

C] To from the grinding wheel shape

D] To hold the abrasive grains and to form the wheel shape

INDUSTRIAL TRAINING INSTITUTE

Monthly Test-7, Marks- 20, Date:- ______________

(Every Question Carry Two Marks)

1-101] given grit size of grinding wheel 46, select suitable grinding operation ----------

A] For pedestal grinding used for edge preparation in welder shop

B] For both roughing and finishing of hardened job on surface grinder

C] For roughing operation on surface grinder

D] To be used in cylindrical grinder

2-102] For grinding operation which grit size of grinding wheel is suitable for re sharpening the

blunt single point tools on bench grinder finishing operation ----------

A] 36

B] 46

C] 60

D] 80

3-103] in grinding operation, for grinding softer materials --------

A] Coarser grain size is used

B] Fin grain size is used

C] Medium grain size is used

D] Any grain size may be used

4-104] Open structured wheel is used for ----------

A] Better cooling is required

B] High work speed

C] Rough finishing

D] Light and old machine

5-105] The structure of the grinding wheel depends upon --------

A] Hardness of the material being ground

B] Nature of the grinding operation

C] Finish required

D] All of these (v] Grade

6-106] Soft wheel is used when

A] The stock of material to be removed is heavier cut

B] High finish required

C] Area of contact is more

D] Grinding hard materials

7-107] me grade or grinding wheel depends on.................

A] Softness

B] Hardness

C] Brittleness

D] Porosity

8-108] ln grinding practice, the term hardness of the wheel or grade of the wheel" refers to --------

A] Hardness of the abrasives used

B] Strength of the bond of the wheel

C] Hardness of the work piece

D] Type of abrasive used

9-109] Standard shapes of a grinding wheel are designated by ----------

A] Types of number

B] Types of grains

C] Types of wheels

D] Types of shapes

10-110] Relict holes provided in the work piece are to accommodate the sharp -----------of the

grinding wheel.

A] Corner

B] Middle

C] Cross

D] Parallel to face

INDUSTRIAL TRAINING INSTITUTE

Monthly Test-8, Marks- 20, Date:- ______________

(Every Question Carry Two Marks)

1-116] A grinding wheel specification is given as 51-A-46-H-5-V-S in which number 46 stands for ----

A] Grade

B] Bond

C] Grain size

D] Structure

2-117] in specification of grinding wheel 51 A -46 -L 5 -V -23, A represent --------

A] Bond type

B] Abrasive type

C] Grain size

D] Bond grade

3-118, A grinding wheel is complete specified by the followmg elements take

A] Type of Abrasive, Grain size, Grade, Structure, Bond

B] Grain size, Grade, Structure, Type of Abrasive, Bond

C] Structure, Bond, Grain size, Type of Abrasive, Grade

D] None of the above

4-119] The stock of the material to be removed is more with heavy cut, we use --------

A] Soft wheel

B] Coarse grain open structure and hard grade wheel

C] Fine grain and dense structure

D] Soft grade and Coarse gram wheel

5-120} Fine grit, hard grade grinding wheel requires -----------grinding allowances than coarse soft grade wheels

A] Leis

B] More

C] Equal

D] None of the above

6-121] For grinding hard material ----------

A] Line grains and dense structure

B] Soft grade and coarse grain wheel

C] Soft wheel.

D] Coarse grain open structure and hard grade wheel

7-122] Soft grade and coarse grain wheel ---------

A] Low work speed

B] Area of contact is more select

C] For grinding hard materials
D] High finish requires
8-123] High finish requires -------
A] Soft grade and coarse grain wheel
B] Soft wheel
C] Fine grain and dense structure
D] Coarse grain open structure and hard grade wheel
9-124] Hard grade and dense structure wheel ----------
A] High wheel speed
B] Rough finish
C] For light and old machine
D] If better cooling is required
10-125] Rough finish -----------' the open structure
A] Open structured wheel
B] Coarse gram an
C] nags wheel
D] Hard grade and dense structure and structure wheel

INDUSTRIAL TRAINING INSTITUTE

Monthly Test-9, Marks- 20, Date:- ______________

(Every Question Carry Two Marks)

1-131] Name the geometrical test of mandrel shown in figure.
A] Check for ovality
B] Check for taper
C] Check for eccentric
D] Check for concentric
2-132] ISO 9000 pertains to ....
Productivity
B] Safety cleanliness
C] Cleanliness
D] Updating the records
3-133] The first spark should be pick up at -----
A] Right hand end of work
B] Left hand end work
C] The middle of work
D] The high spot of the work
4-134] Grinding wheel balancing is required for ------
A] Turning the wheel
B] To remove more material

C] Minimize the machine vibration during grinding

D] To run at higher speed

5-137] 'B' type centre is provided on mandrel is ----------------‘

A] To engagement of centre support

B] To drive the mandrel

C] To protect the centre from damage

D] To reduce the weight 0 e

6-139] Collar type mandrels are used for checking of ------

A] Bore type component

B] Shaft type component

C] Bore with seating face component

D] Face seating component

7-140] Collets are made out of ----------

A] Mild steel

B] Tool steel

C] Spring steel

D] Construction steel

8-141] To expose new position to the grinding wheel, the diamond point should be turned to --form its previous position. 0

A] 60°

B] 90°

C] 45°

D] 30

9-142] If this operation is done frequently the wheel life becomes shorter d.

A] Glazing

B] Truing

C] Dressing

D] Loa mg

10-145] The process of equalizing the centrifugal force developed during grinding ---------

A] Glazing

B] Truing

C] Loading

D] Dressing

INDUSTRIAL TRAINING INSTITUTE

Monthly Test-10, Marks- 20, Date:- _______________

(Every Question Carry Two Marks)

1-151] A grinding wheel gets glazed due to --------

A] Wear of abrasive grains

B] Wear of bond

C] Cracks in wheel

D] Sharpening of wheel

2-152] Dry grinding requires --------grinding allowance than wet grinding.

A] Less

B] Equal

C] More

D] None of these

3-153] The advantage of wet grinder is ------------

A] Dust extractor requirement

B] Grinding wheel wears faster

C] Flying particle are spoil the atmosphere

D] Grinding operation able to control effectively

4-154] Purpose of using the coolant in grinding operation is ------

A] To reduce the heat of work

B] To reduce the heat of wheel

C] To reduce the heat of wheel and carry away the grinding dust

D] to maintain the machine temperature

5-155] water and paraffin mixed coolant is used for diamond wheel grinder the mixture ratio of coolant is……

A] 1:1

B] 1:2

C] 123

D] 1:4

6-156] What is the coolant mixing ratio of soluble oil and water to use on cast iron and hardened steel metals?

A] 1:20

B] 1:30

C] 1:40

D]1:60

7-157] Coolant retention is affected by the grinding wheel's --------

A] Hardness

B] Bond type

C] Grain size

D] Porosity

8-158] Which one of the following is not a property of cutting fluid?

A] Low specific heat

B] High lubricity

D] Chemical stability

C] High film boiling point

9-159] Extreme pressure additive (EPA] is mixed with cutting fluid for improving its power of.

A] Cooling

B] Lubrication

D] Production of the machined surface

C] Cleaning of cutting zone

10-160] The main purpose for using a lubricant in machine tools is to ------

A] Cool down the making parts

B] Prevent machine tool from heating

C] Wet the making parts for close contact

D] Minimize the friction between the making parts

INDUSTRIAL TRAINING INSTITUTE

Monthly Test-11, Marks- 20, Date:- ______________

(Every Question Carry Two Marks)

1-381] For face copying........] Type template is used

A] Rounded

B] Plate type

C] Flat

D] Triangular

2-382]............] Is Main principle of CNC MACHINE?

A] Indicate all states in numbers

B] More time required for mechanical control on machine.

C] Cutting speed is more than manual control.

D] Production sequence in workshop is stored by block number in machine.

3-383] For copy of one shaft.......] Type template is used.

A] Rounded

B] Triangular

C] Flats

D] Square

4-384] The symptoms of continuous path is

A] Called counting system.

B] Tool and work piece on co-ordinate Axis for inter related motion.

C] By the setting of cutter feed and speed

D] Above all

5-385] Misc command M30 means........

A] End of program and reset

B] Program stop

C] Clockwise motion of spindle

D] Complete the programs

6-386] Following which affect on milling surface while by milling with unsetting spindle vertical milling machine with- longitudinal feed.

A] Convex surface

B] Concave surface

C] Radius cross line

D] Rough surface

7-387] While milling by vertical milling machine with 12 mm dia end mill cutter through slot provide on mild steel plate the cutter is sleep and broken for this fault how it is avoid.

A] High speed spindle

B] Low cutting speed

C] Increase of cut depth

D] Less the depth and feed of cutter

8-388] Having 5 mm pitch of screw and dividing ratio of 40 : 1 what is lead of milling machine

A] 0.25 mm

B] 5 mm

C] 8 mm

D] 200 mm

9-389] If not use of backlash Eliminator slap cutter used for down milling operation which safety to be observed?

A] Less lead and depth

B] High lead

C] high lead and less depth

D] High lead and high speed

10-390] Zero offset is the distance between.....] And.........

A] G41 & g42

B] Machine zero & work zero

C] Reference point and tapping mode

D] None of them

INDUSTRIAL TRAINING INSTITUTE

Monthly Test-12, Marks- 20, Date:- ______________

(Every Question Carry Two Marks)

1-421] In CNC program which letter is used to indicate TOOL function number of tool

A] T

B] S

C] M

D] F

2-422] In CNC program which miscellaneous function used to program stop

A] M03

B] M00

C] M01

D] M02

3-423] One of the below miscellaneous function used to program optional Stop

A] M 01

B] M 02

C] M 03

D] M 04

4-424] In CNC program miscellaneous function M02 is used to......

A] Program stop

B] Optional program stop

C] End of program

D] Clockwise spindle on

5-425] In CNC program miscellaneous function M03 is used to..........

A] Counter clockwise spindle on

B] Clockwise spindle on

C] Spindle off

D] Tool change

6-426] One of the below miscellaneous function used in CNC program for spindle stop.

A] M04

B] M05

C] M06

D] M07

7-427] In CNC program which miscellaneous function is used for Tools change

A] M06

B] M07

C] M09

D] M10

8-428] One of the below miscellaneous function used in CNC program for coolant on

A] M08

B] M09

C] M10

D] M11

9-429] One of the below miscellaneous function in CNC program used for coolant off

A] M11

B] M10

C] M9

D] M15

10-430] In CNC program which miscellaneous function used for clamping the job on machine table.

A] M09

B] M10

C] M11

D] M15

www.ingramcontent.com/pod-product-compliance
Ingram Content Group UK Ltd.
Pitfield, Milton Keynes, MK11 3LW, UK
UKHW021914190726
13853UKWH00002B/675

9 798886 847352